Woman, Native, Other

WOMAN, NATIVE, OTHER

Writing Postcoloniality and Feminism

Trinh T. Minh-ha

INDIANA UNIVERSITY PRESS

BLOOMINGTON AND INDIANAPOLIS

Manufactured in the United States of America

Library of Congress Cataloging-in-Publication Data

Trinh, T. Minh-Ha (Thi Minh-Ha), 1952–
Woman, native, other.

Bibliography: p.
Includes index.
1. Women authors—20th century. 2. Women and literature. 3. Feminism and literature. 4. Literature, Modern—20th century—History and criticism.
I. Title.
PN471.T75   1989   809'.89287   88-45455
ISBN 0-253-36603-8
ISBN 0-253-20503-4 (pbk.)

1 2 3 4 5 93 92 91 90 89

To my sisters
Le-Hang,
Thu-Thuy,
Ngoc-Quynh,
Ngoc-Diep,
Ngoc-Lan

I would like to thank Margaret Wilkerson for her support while she was directing the Center for the Study, Education, and Advancement of Women at the University of California–Berkeley; Ellen Mathews, Johanna Drucker, and Kate Rothrock Neri for their editing assistance; Jean-Paul for his master's role and displaced comments; and all the women quoted here, whose spoken words and writings have allowed the story to shift, grow, and circulate.

CONTENTS

Woman, Native, Other

The Story Began Long Ago . . .

This is the world in which I move uninvited, profane on a sacred land, neither me nor mine, but me nonetheless. The story began long ago . . . it is old. Older than my body, my mother's, my grandmother's. As old as my me, Old Spontaneous me, the world. For years we have been passing it on, so that our daughters and granddaughters may continue to pass it on. So that it may become larger than its proper measure, always larger than its own in-significance. The story never really begins nor ends, even though there is a beginning and an end to every story, just as there is a beginning and an end to every teller. One can date it back to the immemorial days when a group of mighty men attributed to itself a central, dominating position vis-à-vis other groups; overvalued its particularities and achievements; adopted a projective attitude toward those it classified among the out-groups; and wrapped itself up in its own thinking, interpreting the out-group through the in-group mode of reasoning while claiming to speak the minds of both the in-group and the out-group.

In a remote village, people have decided to get together to discuss certain matters of capital importance to the well-being of their community. A meeting is thus fixed for a definite date at the marketplace at nightfall. On the day and at the time agreed, each member eats, washes her/himself, and arrives only when s/he is ready. Things proceed smoothly as usual, and the discussion does not have to begin at a precise time, since it does not break in on daily village life but slips naturally into it. A mother continues to bathe her child amidst the group; two men go on playing a game they have started; a woman finishes braiding another woman's hair. These activities do not prevent their listening or intervening when necessary. Never does one open the discussion by coming right to the heart of the matter. For the heart of the matter is always somewhere else than where it is supposed to be. To allow it to emerge, people approach it indirectly by postponing until it matures, by letting it come when it is ready to come. There is no catching, no pushing, no directing, no breaking through, no need for a linear progression which gives the comforting illusion that one knows where one goes. Time and space are not something entirely exterior to oneself, something that one has, keeps, saves, wastes, or loses. Thus, even though one meets to discuss, for example, the problem of survival with this year's crops, one begins to speak of so-and-so who has left his wife, children, family, and village in search of a job in the city and has not given any news since then, or of the neighbor's goats which have eaten so-and-so's millet. The conversation moves from the difficulties caused by rural depopulation to the need to construct goat pens, then wanders in old sayings and remembrances of events that occurred long ago . . . A man starts singing softly and playing his lute. Murmurs, laughter, and snatches of conversation mingle under the moonlight. Some women drowse on a mat they have spread on the ground and wake up when they are spoken to. The discussion lingers on late into the night. By the end of the meeting, everyone has spoken. The chief of the village does not "have the floor" for himself, nor does he talk more than anyone else. He is there to listen, to absorb, and to ascertain at the close what everybody has already felt or grown to feel during the session.

The story never stops beginning or ending. It appears headless and bottomless for it is built on differences. Its (in)finitude subverts every notion of completeness and its frame remains a non-totalizable one. The differences it brings about are differences not only in structure, in the play of structures and of surfaces, but also in timbre and in silence. We—you and me, she and he, we and they—we differ in the content of the words, in the construction and weaving of sentences but most of all, I feel, in the choice and mixing of utterances, the ethos, the tones, the paces, the cuts, the pauses. The story circulates like a gift; an empty gift which anybody can lay claim to by filling it to taste, yet can never truly possess. A gift built on multiplicity. One that stays inexhaustible within its own limits. Its departures and arrivals. Its quietness.

Its quietness. As our elder Lao Tzu used to say, knowing ignorance is strength, ignoring knowledge is sickness; if one is sick of sickness, then one is no longer sick. For a variation, I would say knowledge for knowledge's sake is sickness. Let her who is sick with sickness pass on the story, a gift unasked for like a huge bag of moonlight. Now stars shine white on a black on a colored sky.

"May my story be beautiful and unwind like a long thread . . . ," she recites as she begins her story. A story that stays inexhaustible within its own limits (Stills from **I-C**)

I

Commitment from the Mirror-Writing Box

A grain of sand contains all land and sea
> —Zen saying

"poetic language" . . . is an unsettling process—when not an outright destruction—of the identity of meaning and speaking subject, and consequently, of transcendence or, by derivation, of "religious sensitivity."
> —Julia Kristeva, Desire in Language

i was made to believe
we who write also dance
yet no dancer writes
(the way we write)
no writer ever dances
(the way they dance)
while writing we bend
and bend over
stoop sit and squat
and can neither stand erect
nor lie flat on our back
whoever pretends to feed
walk skip run while writing
must be flying free
as free as a cage-bird
seeing not lines as lines
bars as bars
nor any prison-yard

All stills are taken from the following films by Trinh T. Minh-ha: *Reassemblage* (R); *Naked Spaces—Living Is Round* (NS); *Surname Viet Given Name Nam* (SVGNN); *India—China* (work in progress) (I-C). The production photographs are by Jean-Paul Bourdier.

The triple bind

Neither black/red/yellow nor woman but poet or writer. For many of us, the question of priorities remains a crucial issue. Being merely "a writer" without doubt ensures one a status of far greater weight than being "a woman of color who writes" ever does. Imputing race or sex to the creative act has long been a means by which the literary establishment cheapens and discredits the achievements of non-mainstream women writers. She who "happens to be" a (non-white) Third World member, a woman, and a writer is bound to go through the ordeal of exposing her work to the abuse of praises and criticisms that either ignore, dispense with, or overempha-size her racial and sexual attributes. Yet the time has passed when she can confidently identify herself with a profession or artistic vocation without questioning and relating it to her color-woman condition. Today, the growing ethnic-feminist consciousness has made it increasingly difficult for her to turn a blind eye not only to the specification of the writer as historical subject (who writes? and in what context?), but also to writing itself as a practice located at the intersection of subject and history—a literary practice that involves the possible knowledge (linguistical and ideological) of itself as such. On the one hand, no matter what position she decides to take, she will sooner or later find herself driven into situations where she is made to feel she must choose from among three conflicting identities. Writer of color? Woman writer? Or woman of color? Which comes first? Where does she place her loyalties? On the other hand, she often finds herself at odds with language, which partakes in the white-male-is-norm ideology and is used predominantly as a vehicle to circulate established power relations. This is further intensified by her finding herself also at odds with her relation to writing, which when carried out uncritically often proves to be one of domination: as holder of speech, she usually writes from a position of power, creating as an "author," situating herself *above* her work and existing *before* it, rarely simultaneously *with* it. Thus, it has become almost impossible for her to take up her pen without at the same time questioning her relation to the material that defines her and her creative work. As focal point of cultural consciousness and social change, writing weaves into language the complex relations of a subject caught between the problems of race and gender and the practice of literature as the very place where social alienation is thwarted differently according to each specific context.

Silence in time

Writing, reading, thinking, imagining, speculating. These are luxury activities, so I am reminded, permitted to a privileged few, whose idle hours of the day can be viewed otherwise than as a bowl of rice or a loaf of bread less to share with the family. "If we wish to increase the supply of rare and remarkable women like the Brontës," wrote our reputed foresister Virginia Woolf, "we should give the Joneses and the Smiths rooms of their own and five hundred [pounds] a year. One cannot grow fine flowers in a thin soil."[1] Substantial creative achievement demands not necessarily genius, but acumen, bent, persistence, time. And time, in the framework of industrial development, means a wage that admits of leisure and living conditions that do not require that writing be incessantly interrupted, deferred, denied, at any rate subordinated to family responsibilities. "When the claims of creation cannot be primary," Tillie Olsen observes, "the results are atrophy; unfinished work; minor effort and accomplishment; silences." The message Olsen conveys in *Silences* leaves no doubt as to the circumstances under which most women writers function. It is a constant reminder of those who never come to writing: "the invisible, the as-innately-capable: the born to the wrong circumstances—diminished, excluded, foundered."[2] To say this, however, is not to say that writing should be held in veneration in all milieus or that every woman who fails to write is a disabled being. (What Denise Paulme learned in this regard during her first period of fieldwork in Africa is revealing. Comparing her life one day with those of the women in an area of the French Sudan, she was congratulating herself on not having to do a chore like theirs—pounding millet for the meals day in and day out—when she overheard herself commented upon by one of the women nearby: "That girl makes me tired with her everlasting paper and pencil: what sort of a life is that?" The lesson, Paulme concluded, "was a salutary one, and I have never forgotten it.")[3] To point out that, in general, the situation of women does not favor literary productivity is to imply that it is almost impossible for them (and especially for those bound up with the Third World) to engage in writing as an occupation without their letting themselves be consumed by a deep and pervasive sense of guilt. Guilt over the selfishness implied in such activity, over themselves as housewives and "women," over their families, their friends, and all other "less fortunate" women. The circle in which they turn proves to be vicious, and writing in such a context is always practiced at the cost of other women's labor. Doubts, lack of confidence, frustrations, despair: these are sentiments born with the habits of distraction, distortion, discontinuity, and silence. After having toiled for a number of years on her book, hattie gossett exclaims to herself:

> Who do you think you are [to be writing a book]? and who cares what you think about anything enough to pay money for it . . . a major portion of your audience not only cant read but seems to think readin is a waste of time? plus books like this arent sold in the ghetto bookshops or even in airports?[4]

The same doubt is to be heard through Gloria Anzaldúa's voice:

> Who gave us permission to perform the act of writing? Why does writing
> seem so unnatural for me? . . . The voice recurs in me: *Who am I, a poor
> Chicanita from the sticks, to think I could write?* How dared I even consider
> becoming a writer as I stooped over the tomato fields bending, bending
> under the hot sun. . . .
> How hard it is for us to *think* we can choose to become writers, much less *feel*
> and *believe* that we can.[5]

Rites of passage

S/he who writes, writes. In uncertainty, in necessity. And does not ask
whether s/he is given the permission to do so or not. Yet, in the context of
today's market-dependent societies, "to be a writer" can no longer mean
purely to perform the act of writing. For a laywo/man to enter the priest-
hood—the sacred world of writers—s/he must fulfill a number of unwritten
conditions. S/he must undergo a series of rituals, be baptized and
ordained. S/he must *submit* her writings to the law laid down by the
corporation of literary/literacy victims and be prepared to *accept* their ver-
dict. Every woman who writes and wishes to become established as a
writer has known the taste of *rejection.* Sylvia Plath's experience is often
cited. Her years of darkness, despair, and disillusion, her agony of slow
rebirth, her moments of fearsome excitement at the start of the writing of
The Bell Jar, her unsuccessful attempts at re-submitting her first book of
poems under ever-changing titles, and the distress with which she up-
braided herself are parts of the realities that affect many women writers:

> Nothing stinks like a pile of unpublished writing, which remark I guess
> shows I still don't have a pure motive (O it's-such-fun-I-just-can't-stop-who-
> cares-if-it's-published-or-read) about writing. . . . I still want to see it finally
> ritualized in print.[6]

Accumulated unpublished writings do stink. They heap up before your
eyes like despicable confessions that no one cares to hear; they sap your
self-confidence by incessantly reminding you of your failure to incorporate. For publication means the breaking of a first seal, the end of a
"no-admitted" status, the end of a soliloquy confined to the private sphere,
and the start of a possible sharing with the unknown other—the reader,
whose collaboration with the writer alone allows the work to come into full
being. Without such a rite of passage, the woman-writer-to-be/woman-to-
be-writer is condemned to wander about, begging for permission to join in

and be a member. If it is difficult for any woman to find acceptance for her writing, it is all the more so for those who do not match the stereotype of the "real woman"—the colored, the minority, the physically or mentally handicapped. Emma Santos, who spent her days running to and fro between two worlds—that of hospitals and that of the "normal" system—equally rejected by Psychiatry and by Literature, is another writer whose first book has been repeatedly dismissed (by twenty-two publishing houses). Driven to obsession by a well-known publisher who promised to send her an agreement but never did, she followed him, spied on him, called him twenty times a day on the phone, and ended up feeling like "a pile of shit making after great men of letters." Writing, she remarks, is "a shameful, venereal disease," and Literature, nothing more than "a long beseeching." Having no acquaintance, no friend to introduce her when she sought admission for her work among the publishers, she describes her experience as follows:

> I receive encouraging letters but I am goitrous. Publishers, summons, these are worse than psychiatrists, interrogatories. The publishers perceive a sick and oblivious girl. They would have liked the text, the same one, without changing a single word, had it been presented by a young man from the [Ecole] Normale Superieure, *agrégé* of philosophy, worthy of the Goncourt prize.[7]

The Guilt

To capture a publisher's attention, to convince, to negotiate: these constitute one step forward into the world of writers, one distress, one guilt. One guilt among the many yet to come, all of which bide their time to loom up out of their hiding places, for the path is long and there is an ambush at every turn. Writing: not letting it merely haunt you and die over and over again in you until you no longer know how to speak. Getting published: not loathing yourself, not burning it, not giving up. Now I (the all-knowing subject) feel almost secure with such definite "not-to-do's." Yet, I/i (the plural, non-unitary subject) cannot set my mind at rest with them without at the same time recognizing their precariousness. i (the personal race- and gender-specific subject) have, in fact turned a deaf ear to a number of primary questions: Why write? For whom? What necessity? What writing? What impels you and me and hattie gossett to continue to write when we know for a fact that our books are not going to be "sold in the ghetto bookshops or even in airports?" And why do we care for their destinations at all? "A writer," proclaims Toni Cade Bambara, "like any other cultural worker, like any other member of the community, ought to try to put her/his skills in the service of the community." It is apparently on account of such a conviction that Bambara "began a career as the neighborhood scribe," helping people write letters to faraway relatives as well as letters of complaint, petitions, contracts, and the like.[8] For those of us who call ourselves "writers" in the context of a community whose major portion "not only cant read but seems to think readin is a waste of time" (gossett), being "the neighborhood scribe" is no doubt one of the most gratifying and unpretentious ways of dedicating oneself to one's people. Writing as a social function—as differentiated from the ideal of art for art's sake—is the aim that Third World writers, in defining their roles, highly esteem and claim. *Literacy* and *literature* intertwine so tightly, indeed, that the latter has never ceased to imply both the ability to read and the condition of being well read—and thereby to convey the sense of *polite learning* through the arts of *grammar* and *rhetoric*. The illiterate, the ignorant versus the wo/man of "letters" (of wide reading), the highly educated. With such discrimination and opposition, it is hardly surprising that the writer should be viewed as a social parasite. Whether s/he makes common cause with the upper classes or chooses to disengage her/himself by adopting the myth of the bohemian artist, the writer is a kept wo/man who for her/his living largely relies on the generosity of that portion of society called the literate. A room of one's own and a pension of five hundred pounds per year solely for making ink marks on paper: this, symbolically speaking, is what many people refer to when they say the writer's activity is "gratuitous" and "useless." No matter how devoted to the vocation s/he may be, the writer cannot subsist on words and mere fresh air, nor can s/he really "live by the pen," since her/his work—arbitrarily estimated as it is—has no definite market value. Reading in this context may actually prove to be "a waste of time," and writing, as Woolf puts it, "a reputable and harmless occupation." Reflecting on her profession as a writer (in a 1979 interview), Toni Cade Bambara noted that she probably did not begin "getting really serious about writing until maybe five years ago. Prior to that, in spite of all good sense, I always thought writing was rather frivolous, that it was something you did because you didn't feel like doing any work." The concept of "writing" here seems to be incompatible with the concept of "work." As the years went by and Toni Cade Bambara got more involved in writing, however, she changed her attitude and has "come to appreciate that it is a perfectly legitimate way to participate in struggle."[9]

Commitment as an ideal is particularly dear to Third World writers. It helps to alleviate the Guilt: that of being privileged (Inequality), of "going over the hill" to join the clan of literates (Assimilation), and of indulging in a "useless" activity while most community members "stoop over the tomato fields, bending under the hot sun" (a perpetuation of the same privilege). In a sense, committed writers are the ones who write both to awaken to the consciousness of their guilt and to give their readers a guilty conscience. Bound to one another by an awareness of their guilt, writer and reader may thus assess their positions, engaging themselves wholly in their situations and carrying their weight into the weight of their communities, the weight of the world. Such a definition naturally places the committed writers on the side of Power. For every discourse that breeds fault and guilt is a discourse of authority and arrogance. To say this, however, is not to say that all power discourses produce equal oppression or that those established are necessary. Discussing African literature and the various degrees of propaganda prompted by commitment, Ezekiel Mphahlele observes that although "propaganda is always going to be with us"—for "there will always be the passionate outcry against injustice, war, fascism, poverty"—the manner in which a writer protests reflects to a large extent her/his regard for the reader and "decides the literary worth of a work." "Commitment," Mphahlele adds, "need not give rise to propaganda: the writer can make [her/]his stand known without advocating it . . . in two-dimensional terms, i.e., in terms of one response to one stimulus."[10] Thus, in the whirlwind of prescriptive general formula such as: Black art must "respond *positively* to the reality of revolution" or Black art must "expose the enemy, *praise* the people, and *support* the revolution" (Ron Karenga, my italics), one also hears distinct, unyielding voices whose autonomy asserts itself as follows:

> Black pride need not blind us to our own weaknesses: in fact it should help us to perceive our weaknesses. . . .
> I do not care for black pride that drugs us into a condition of stupor and inertia. I do not care for it if leaders use it to dupe the masses.[11]

> To us, the man who adores the Negro is as sick as the man who abominates him.[12]

Freedom and the masses

The notion of *art engagé* as defined by Jean-Paul Sartre, an influential apologist for socially effective literature, continues to grow and to circulate among contemporary engaged writers. It is easy to find parallels (and it is often directly quoted) in Third World literary discourses. "A free man addressing free men," the Sartrian writer "has only one subject— freedom." He writes to "appeal to the reader's freedom to collaborate in the production of his work" and paints the world "only so that free men may feel their freedom as they face it."[13] The function of literary art, in other words, must be to remind us of that freedom and to defend it. Made to serve a political purpose, literature thus places itself within the context of the proletarian fight, while the writer frees himself from his dependence on elites—or in a wider sense, from any privilege—and creates, so to speak, an art for an unrestricted public known as "art for the masses." From the chain of notions dear to Sartre—choice, responsibility, contingency, situation, motive, reason, being, doing, having—two notions are set forth here as being most relevant to Third World engaged literary theories: freedom and the masses. What is freedom in writing? And what can writing-for-the-masses be? Reflecting on being a writer, "female, black, and free," Margaret Walker, for example, defines freedom as "a philosophical state of mind and existence." She proudly affirms:

> My entire career in writing . . . is determined by these immutable facts of my human condition. . . .
> Writing is my life, but it is an avocation nobody can buy. In this respect I believe I am a free agent, stupid perhaps, but *me* and still free. . . .
> The writer is still in the avant-garde for Truth and Justice, for Freedom, Peace, and Human Dignity. . . . Her place, let us be reminded, is anywhere she chooses to be, doing what she has to do, creating, healing, and always being herself.[14]

These lines agree perfectly with Sartre's ideal of liberty. They may be said to echo his concepts of choice and responsibility—according to which each person, being an absolute choice of self, an absolute emergence at an absolute date, must assume her/his situation with the proud consciousness of being the author of it. (For one is nothing but this "being-in-situation" that is the total contingency of the world, of one's birth, past, and environment, and of the fact of one's fellow wo/man.) By its own rationale, such a sense of responsibility (attributed to the lucid, conscientious, successful man of action) renders the relationship between freedom and commitment particularly problematic. Is it not, indeed, always in the name of freedom that My freedom hastens to stamp out those of others? Is it not also in the name of the masses that My personality bestirs itself to impersonalize those of my fellow wo/men? Do the masses become masses by themselves? Or are they the result of a theoretical and practical operation of "massification"? From where onward can one say of a "free" work of art that it is written for the infinite numbers which constitute the masses and not merely for a definite public stratum of society?

For the people, by the people, and from the people

Like all stereotypical notions, the notion of the masses has both an upgrading connotation and a degrading one. One often speaks of the masses as one speaks of the people, magnifying thereby their number, their strength, their mission. One invokes them and pretends to write on their behalf when one wishes to give weight to one's undertaking or to justify it. The Guilt mentioned earlier is always lurking below the surface. Yet to oppose the masses to the elite is already to imply that those forming the masses are regarded as an aggregate of average persons condemned by their lack of personality or by their dim individualities to stay with the herd, to be docile and anonymous. Thus the notion of "art *for* the masses" supposes not only a split between the artist and her/his audience—the spectator-consumer—but also a passivity on the part of the latter. For art here is not attributed to the masses; it is ascribed to the active few, whose role is precisely to produce *for* the great numbers. This means that despite the shift of emphasis the elite-versus-masses opposition remains intact. In fact it must remain so, basically unchallenged, if it is to serve a conservative political and ideological purpose—in other words, if (what is defined as) "art" is to exist at all. One of the functions of this "art for the masses" is, naturally, to contrast with the other, higher "art for the elite," and thereby to enforce its elitist values. The wider the distance between the two, the firmer the stand of conservative art. One can no longer let oneself be deceived by concepts that oppose the artist or the intellectual to the masses and deal with them as with two incompatible entities. Criticisms arising from or dwelling on such a *myth* are, indeed, quite commonly leveled against innovators and more often used as tools of intimidation than as reminders of social interdependency. It is perhaps with this perspective in mind that one may better understand the variants of Third World literary discourse, which claims not exactly an "art for the masses," but an "art for the people, by the people, and from the people." In an article on "Le Poète noir et son peuple" (The Black Poet and His People), for example, Jacques Rabemananjara virulently criticized Occidental poets for spending their existence indulging in aesthetic refinements and subtleties that bear no relation to their peoples' concerns and aspirations, that are merely sterile intellectual delights. The sense of dignity, Rabemananjara said, forbids black Orpheus to go in for the cult of art for art's sake. Inspirer inspired by his people, the poet has to play the difficult role of being simultaneously the torch lighting the way for his fellowmen and their loyal interpreter. "He is more than their spokesman: he is their voice": his noble mission entitles him to be "not only the messenger, but the very message of his people."[15] The concept of a popular and functional art is here poised against that of an intellectual and aesthetic one. A justified regression? A shift of emphasis again? Or an attempt at fusion of the self and the other, of art, ideology, and life? Let us listen to other, perhaps less didactic voices; that of Aimé Césaire in *Return to My Native Land:*

"Poetry is the culture of a people. We are poets even when we don't write poems . . ." (Nikki Giovanni) (Stills: above from **I-C**; below from **NS**)

I should come back to this land of mine and say to it: "Embrace me without fear. . . . If all I can do is speak, at least I shall speak for you."
And I should say further: "My tongue shall serve those miseries which have no tongue, my voice the liberty of those who founder in the dungeons of despair."
And I should say to myself: "And most of all beware, even in thought, of assuming the sterile attitude of the spectator, for life is not a spectacle, a sea of griefs is not a proscenium, a man who wails is not a dancing bear. "[16]

that of Nikki Giovanni in *Gemini:*

Poetry is the culture of a people. We are poets even when we don't write poems. . . . We are all preachers because we are One. . . . I don't think we younger poets are doing anything significantly different from what we as a people have always done. The new Black poetry is in fact just a manifestation of our collective historical needs.[17]

and that of Alice Walker in an essay on the importance of models in the artist's life:

It is, in the end, the saving of lives that we writers are about. . . . We do it because we care. . . . We care because we know this: *The life we save is our own.*[18]

One may say of art for art's sake in general that it is itself a reaction against the bourgeois "functional" attitude of mind which sees in the acquisition of art the highest, purest form of consumption. By making explicit the gratuitousness of their works, artists show contempt for their wealthy customers, whose purchasing power allows them to subvert art in its subversiveness, reducing it to a mere commodity or a service. As a reaction, however, art for art's sake is bound to be 'two-dimensional"—"one response to one stimulus" (Mphahlele)—and, therefore, to meet with no success among writers of the Third World. "I cannot imagine," says Wole Soyinka, "that our 'authentic black innocent' would ever have permitted himself to be manipulated into the false position of countering one pernicious Manicheism with another."[19] An art that claims to be at the same time sender and bearer of a message, to serve the people and "to come off the street" (Cade Bambara), should then be altogether "functional, collective, and committing or committed" (Karenga). The reasoning circle closes on the notion of commitment, which again emerges, fraught with questions.

Vertically imposed language: on clarity, craftsmanship, and She who steals language

When commitment remains limited to the sociopolitical sphere, the claim of a "functional" writing that advocates the cause of the oppressed and instructs its audience indicates, in Mphahlele's terms, "a dangerous tendency." It tends "to draw a line of distinction between a function in which an author vindicates or asserts black pride or takes a sociopolitical stand and a function in which he seeks to stir humanity as a whole." For literature, which "takes in wider circles of humanity" even while it particularizes and is an appeal to the freedom in the Sartrian sense of all men and women, such a distinction is bound to be dangerous. "The functions overlap, and the bigger the rift between them the more stridently its propaganda yells out, the more life's ironies and paradoxes are overlooked, and the more the reader feels his sense of belonging assailed or unduly exploited"[20] (Mphahlele). What emerges here are the questions that relate to the nature of literature and writing. On the one hand, can literature be a "freedom that has taken freedom as its end" (Sartre) and still concern itself with elements like structure, form, and style—whose totality precisely allows literature to take on its meaning? On the other hand, can a writing that claims to break down rules and myths submit itself to the exclusive rules of a sociopolitical stand? Nothing could be more normative, more logical, and more authoritarian than, for example, the (politically) revolutionary poetry or prose that speaks of revolution in the form of commands or in the well-behaved, steeped-in-convention-language of "clarity." ("A wholesome, clear, and direct language" is said to be "the fulcrum to move the mass or to sanctify it.")[21] *Clear* expression, often equated with *correct* expression, has long been the criterion set forth in treatises on *rhetoric*, whose aim was to order discourse so as to *persuade*. The language of Taoism and Zen, for example, which is perfectly accessible but rife with paradox does not qualify as "clear" (paradox is "illogical" and "nonsensical" to many Westerners), for its intent lies outside the realm of persuasion. The same holds true for vernacular speech, which is not acquired through institutions—schools, churches, professions, etc.—and therefore not repressed by either grammatical rules, technical terms, or key words. Clarity as a purely rhetorical attribute serves the purpose of a classical feature in language, namely, its instrumentality. To write is to communicate, express, witness, impose, instruct, redeem, or save—at any rate to *mean* and to send out *an unambiguous message*. Writing thus reduced to a mere vehicle of thought may be *used* to orient toward a goal or to sustain an act, but it does not constitute an act in itself. This is how the division between the writer/the intellectual and the activists/the masses becomes possible. To use the language well, says the voice of literacy, cherish its classic form. Do not choose the offbeat at the cost of clarity. Obscurity is an imposition on the reader. True, but beware when you cross railroad tracks for one train may hide another train. Clarity is a means of subjection, a quality both of official, taught language and of correct writing, two old mates of power: together they flow, together they flower, vertically, to impose an order. Let us not forget that writers who advocate the instrumentality of language are often those who cannot or choose not to see the suchness of things—a language as language—and therefore, continue to preach conformity to the norms of well-behaved writing: principles of composition, style, genre, correction, and improvement. To write "clearly," one must incessantly prune, eliminate, forbid, purge, purify; in other words, practice what may be called an "ablution of language" (Roland Barthes).

"Writing for me," says Toni Cade Bambara, "is still an act of language first and foremost."[22] Before being the noble messenger and the loyal message of her/his people, the writer is a wo/man "whose most absorbed and passionate hours are spent arranging words on pieces of paper" (Joan Didion).[23] S/He does not expresses her/his thoughts, passion, or imagination in sentences but *thinks sentences:* she is a sentence-thinker (i.e., "not altogether a thinker and not altogether a sentence parser" [Barthes])[24] who radically questions the world through the questioning of a how-to-write. Drawing attention to the very nature of writing, acknowledging its constraints and artificiality do not, however, necessarily imply laying emphasis on craftsmanship as a criterion for "good" (literary) writing. To substitute a work-value for a use-value is simply to shift from the norms of the clearly written (correct behavior) to those of the well written (patient apprenticeship). The image of the writer as a crafts wo/man who spends regular hours of solitary effort cutting, polishing, and setting her/his form "exactly as a jeweller extracts art from his material"[25] has too often been set forth as the sole determining value. Good writing is thus differentiated from bad writing through a building up of skill and vocabulary and a perfecting of techniques. Since genius cannot be acquired, sophisticated means, skills, and knowledge are dangled before one's eyes as *the* steps to take, *the* ladder to climb if one wishes to come any closer to the top of this monument known as Literature. Invoke the Name. Follow the norms. Of. The Well Written. The master-servant's creed carries on: *you must learn* through patience and discipline. And what counts most is what it costs in *labor* to engender a work, hence the parallel often abusively drawn between the act of writing and the birth process.

> The poet is in labor [Denise Levertov wrote]. She has been told that it will not hurt but it has hurt so much that pain and struggle seem, just now, the only reality. . . . she hears the doctor saying, "Those are the shoulders you are feeling now"—and she knows the head is out then, and the child is pushing and sliding out of her, insistent, a poem.[26]

In her *Journal*, Katherine Mansfield acknowledged:

> What is it that makes the moment of delivery so difficult for me? . . . *Work.*
> Shall I be able to express one day my love of work—my desire to be a better
> writer—my longing to take greater pains. . . . Oh, to be a *writer*, a real writer
> given up to it and to it alone! . . . My deepest desire is to be a writer, to have
> "a body of work" done. . . .[27]

The reflections offered throughout this *Journal* insist on the painstaking
aspects of writing and on moments where Mansfield despaired, over-
whelmed by fear of *failing,* of not *working* regularly enough, in other words,
of not meeting the (Good) Writer's requirements. Labor and craft have
become so cherished as values in writing that it suffices to read any
interview, any account of a writer's life, any statement about the creative
process to recognize how highly prized they remain. Invited to speak for a
course on "How the Writer Writes," Flannery O'Connor observes:

> there is no such thing as THE writer. . . .
> But there is a widespread curiosity about writers and how they work. . . .
> [People] are interested in being a writer, not in writing. . . . And they seem
> to feel that this can be accomplished by learning certain things about work-
> ing habits. . . .[28]

To write well, in this framework of mind, is to arrange the signs of literary
conventions so as to reach an optimum form to "express" a reality—such
as, for example, the self (hence the concept of art as self-expression), which
is often taken for something given, as solid, as referable as an object that
lies deeply hidden under my layers of artificialities, waiting patiently to be
uncovered and proven. Yet I-the-writer do not *ex*press (a) reality more than
(a) reality *im*presses itself on me. Expresses me. The function of the
craftswo/man-writer is, therefore, "not so much to create a work as to
supply a literature which can be seen from afar" (Barthes). The display of
craftsmanship, when assumed clear-sightedly however, is a self-
confessed, sometimes self-reflexive, form of art for art's sake that holds
pragmatic bourgeois activity up to ridicule and, at best, invalidates it. By
laying bare the codes of literary labor, it unequivocally acknowledges the
writer's contradictory stand—her being condemned to do "good work" in
choosing to "write well" and to produce Literature. *She writes,* finally not to
express, nor so much to materialize an idea or a feeling, as *to possess and
dispossess herself of the power of writing.* Bliss.

"A lady of letters, what a funny expression . . . ," says Simone de
Beauvoir in an interview with Jean-Paul Sartre, who wonders what it feels
like in life to be such a lady (creature). To write is to become. Not to

become a writer (or a poet), but to become, intransitively. Not when writing adopts established keynotes or policy, but when it traces for itself lines of evasion. Can any one of us write *like* a man, *like* a woman, *like* a white? Surely, someone would quickly answer, and this leads us straight back to the old master-servant's Guilt. A sentence-thinker, yes, but one who so very often does not know how a sentence will end, I say. And as there is no need to rush, just leave it open, so that it may later on find, or not find, its closure. Words, fragments, and lines that I love for no sound reason; blanks, lapses, and silences that settle in like gaps of fresh air as soon as the inked space smells stuffy. Learned women have often been described in terms one might use in describing a thief. Being able to read and write, a learned woman robs man of his creativity, his activity, his culture, his language. Learning "unfeminizes." Thus, Lady Murasaki picked up Chinese by eavesdropping on her brother's lessons but was careful to conceal her knowledge. Pretending she could not understand a single character of this language, she wrote only in Japanese. It was, indeed, less of an encroachment upon male privilege to write in the *native* language, which learned men of eleventh-century Japan considered to be vulgar (therefore, a language suitable for a woman or a commoner). The French seventeenth-century Madame Lafayette, who studied Latin in secret (therefore stole culture) and whose maiden name was de La Vergne, was associated with Lavernia, the Roman goddess of theft. On the other hand, Anaïs Nin, who was most eager to "protect men, not [to] outshine them," and forbade herself to disclose her powers, arrived at the following observations in her *Diary:*

> Had guilt suffocated my work? . . . Guilt. guilt everywhere. . . . I did not want to steal man's creation, his thunder. Creation and femininity seem incompatible. The *aggressive* act of creation. . . .
> I have crippled myself.
> Dreams of Chinese women with bound feet. . . .
> Guilt about exposing the father.
> Secrets.
> Need of disguises.[29]

Women writers are both prompt to hide in (their) writing(s) and feel prompted to do so. As language-stealers, they must yet learn to steal without being seen, and with no pretense of being a stealer, for fear of "exposing the father." Such a reluctance to say aloud that the emperor has no clothes and therefore to betray or admit of an evidence comes perhaps less from a subjection to man than from an acute awareness of emptiness— emptiness through (his) power, through (his) language, through (his) disguises. Hence the compassion and the desire to protect. By countering a (masculine) disguise with another (feminine) disguise, however, Nin felt she had crippled herself. Double mischief: unspoken and unable to speak, woman in exile with herself. Stolen language will always remain that other's language. Say it obliquely, use trickery, cheat, or fake, for if I tell you now what I would like to hear myself tell you, I will miss it. Words thoroughly invested with realities that turn out to be not-quite-not-yet-mines are radically deceptive. Whenever I *try my best* to say, I never fail to utter the wrong words; I weasel, telling you "hen" when I mean something close to "duck." "It is useless," Virginia Woolf wrote, "to go to the great men writers for help, however much one may go to them for pleasure. . . . The ape is too distant to be sedulous. Perhaps the first thing she would find, setting pen to paper, was that there was no common sentence ready for her use." A man's sentence is bound to be unsuited for a woman's use; and no matter how splendid her gift for prose proves to be, she will stumble and fall with such a "clumsy weapon in her hands." "Moreover, a book is not made of sentences laid end to end, but of sentences built, if an image helps, into arcades or domes. And this shape too has been made by men out of their own needs for their own uses."[30] *Literally*, she blabs and cackles and is well known as Ms. Tittle-tattle, always willing to sell off for a song what she has stolen (overheard) from man. *Figuratively*, she goes unheard (even when she yells and especially when she "shrills," as they put it) and remains as dumb as a fish. So where do you go from here? where do I go? and where does a committed woman writer go? Finding a voice, searching for words and sentences: say some thing, one thing, or no thing; tie/untie, read/unread, discard their forms; scrutinize the grammatical habits of your writing and decide for yourself whether they free or repress. Again, order(s). Shake syntax, smash the myths, and if you lose, slide on, *unearth* some new linguistic paths. Do you surprise? Do you shock? Do you have a choice?

A sketched window on the world

It is said that the writer's choice is always a two-way choice. Whether one assumes it clear-sightedly or not, by writing one situates oneself vis-à-vis both society and the nature of literature, that is to say, the tools of creation. The way I encounter or incorporate the former, in other words, is the way I confront merge into the latter, for these are the two inseparable faces of a single entity. Neither entirely personal nor purely historical, a mode of writing is in itself a function. An act of historical solidarity, it denotes, in addition to the writer's personal standpoint and intention, a relationship between creation and society. Dealing exclusively with either one of these two aspects, therefore, proves vain as an approach. So does the preaching of revolution through a writing more concerned with imposing than raising consciousness regarding the process by which language works or regarding the nature, activity, and status of writing itself. No radical change can occur as long as writing is not recognized, precisely, as "the choice of that social area within which the writer elects to situate the Nature of her/his language."[31] This calls for a conception of writing that can no longer naïvely be reduced to a *means* of expressing a reality or emitting a message. To lay emphasis on *expression* and on *message* is to forget that even if art is said to be a "window on the world," it is only "a sketched window" (V. Shklovsky). And, just as sketched windows have their own realities, writing as a system by itself has its own rules and structuring process. The *abc* lesson says that for letters to become words and for words to take on meanings, they must relate to other letters, to other words, to the context in which they evolve—be it verbal or non-verbal—as well as to other present *and* absent contexts. (Words are think-tanks loaded with second- and third-order memories that die hard despite their ever-changing meanings.) Thus, writing constantly refers to writing, and no writing can ever claim to be "free" of other writings. When asked why they write, writers usually answer that they do so to create a world of their own, make order out of chaos, heighten their awareness of life, transcend their existences, discover themselves, communicate their feelings, or speak to others. Some add that they write as they breathe, as they stay alive, or as "birds sing," to unfold "the comings and goings of a desire" and "exhaust a task that bears in itself its own bliss." At times Writing is considered as a substitute for something lying *beyond it*, at other times as a necessity and an activity in its own right, devoid of any ulterior motive or any finality. Again, two faces of the same coin. In defining writing, I must acknowledge the mutual dependence of these two aspects if I am to avoid taking the partial for the absolute. The emphasis laid on the notion of writing as (self-)expression offers a good example of such a distortion. In the desperate search for what Susan Griffin calls "the place in myself where words have authority, some true and untouched place that does not mutter what has been said before . . . and make in the very telling a proof of authenticity,"[32] there is a tendency, which many of us share, to confuse the footprints (be they fresh or worn out) made by the shoes with the shoes themselves. The writer here insists on her reluctance to repeat what has been said before and to accept "that there is no purpose . . . no intrinsic authority to my own words." She insists on her feeling of love and despair toward language, on her struggle to arrive at a certain "proof of authenticity," and thereby on her illusory belief in the existence of a redeeming wholeness about which she and I can once and for all have concrete knowledge. Yet it seems obvious that writing does not express any more than it "in-expresses" or "mis-expresses." Having always traced its own limits while going beyond the limits of its assigned role as expression or communication, it may be viewed as that which does not translate a reality outside itself but, more precisely, allows the emergence of a new reality.

The infinite play of empty mirrors (reversed)

Writing necessarily refers to writing. The image is that of a mirror capturing only the reflections of other mirrors. When i say "I see myself seeing myself," I/i am not alluding to the illusory relation of subject to subject (or object) but to the play of mirrors that defers to infinity the real subject and subverts the notion of an original "I." A writing *for* the people, *by* the people, and *from* the people is, literally, a multipolar reflecting reflection that remains free from the conditions of subjectivity and objectivity and yet reveals them both. I write to show myself showing people who show me my own showing. I-You: not one, not two. In this unwonted spectacle made of reality and fiction, where redoubled images form and reform, neither I nor you come first. No primary core of irradiation can be caught hold of, no hierarchical first, second, or *third* exists except as mere illusion. All is empty when one is plural. Yet how difficult it is to keep our mirrors clean. We all tend to cloud and soil them as soon as the older smudges are wiped off, for we love to *use them as instruments* to behold ourselves, maintaining thereby a narcissistic relation of me to me, still me and always me. Rare are the moments when we accept leaving our mirrors empty, even though we may laugh watching our neighbors pining away for their own images. The very error that deceives our eyes inflames them; still, we persist in trying to fix a fleeting image and spend our lifetime searching after that which does not exist. This object we love so, let us just turn away and it will immediately disappear. In the dual relation of subject to subject or subject to object, the mirror is the symbol of an unaltered vision of things. It reveals to me my double, my ghost, my perfections as well as my flaws. Considered an instrument of self-knowledge, one in which I have total faith, it also bears a magical character that has always transcended its functional nature. In this encounter of I with I, the power of identification is often such that reality and appearance merge while the tool itself becomes invisible. Hence the superstitious fear of broken mirrors and the recurring theme (and variations) in Western literature of the poet who smoothly *enters* the mirror for a journey in the dark or the man who, fighting desperately against death, shatters mirror after mirror, only to come again and again, after each attempt at eliminating his reflection, face to face with himself. (To see one's double is to see oneself dead.) From mirage to mirage, the subject/object takes flight and loses its existence. Trying to grasp it amounts to stopping a mirror from mirroring. It is encountering the void. Not a transitory void, but one (the one) that has always been there despite our eternal effort to banish it from conscious sight. A shattered mirror still functions as mirror; it may destroy the dual relation of I to I but leaves the infiniteness of life's reflections intact. Here reality is not reconstituted, it is put into pieces so as to allow another world to rebuild (keep on unbuilding and rebuilding) itself with its debris. Mirrors multiplied and differently disposed are bound to yield fallacious, fairy-like visions, thus constituting a theater of illusions within which countless combinations of reflecting reflections operate. It is by virtue of consciousness of such a mirage-displacement that in Asian cultures the mirror often functions as the "symbol of the very void of symbols." As a Vietnamese monk of the eleventh century said, *"The free man sees all, but nothing is seen by him."* For "the perfect man's mind is like a mirror," Chuang Tzu observed, "it reflects things but does not retain them." Poet, the Shining One . . . s/he who bears such a title receives without ever owning. S/He is blind in the sense of all-seeing and neither communicates nor erases communication. Instead, s/he empties out with each glitter, partaking of that life-giving no thing. When art claims to come only from within *or* from without, it becomes a thing I can rate *first, second,* or *third* (thereby maintaining a hierarchy in the realm of facts). It obstructs light even though it may shine for a time. Should it turn aside at any minute, emptiness will at once leak out/in and the play of infinite mirrors continues. Clarity within, quiet without.

Endless the series of things without name
On the way back to where there is nothing.
They are called shapeless shapes;
Forms without form;
Are called vague semblances.
Go towards them, and you see no front;
Go after them, and you see no rear.

—Lao Tzu, *Tao-te-ching*, 14 (tr. A. Waley)

Writing reflects. It reflects on other writings and, whenever awareness emerges, on itself as writing. Like the Japanese boxes that contain other boxes, nest one inside the other *ad nihilum*,[33] writing is meshing one's writing with the machinery of endless reflexivity. Footprints of emptiness multiplied to infinity in an attempt at disarming death. She says to unsay others so that others may unsay her and say: It's still not it. This circular but still linear reasoning inescapably reduces reality to a chain of causes and effects. It most likely leads to a nihilistic understanding of emptiness, one that tends to define it as a negation of the existence of things. How do you read, for example, the following lines by Katherine Mansfield?

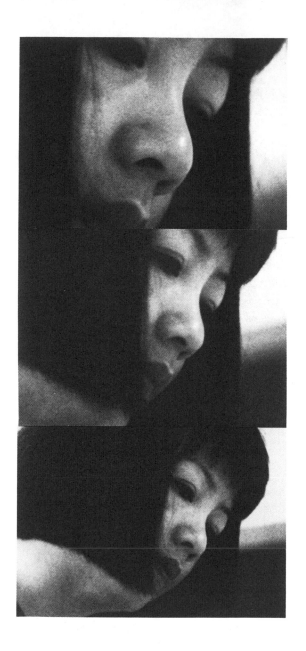

(Stills from **SVGNN**)

Words, fragments, and lines that I love for no sound reason; blanks, lapses, and silences that settle in like gaps of fresh air as soon as the inked space smells stuffy (Stills from **NS**)

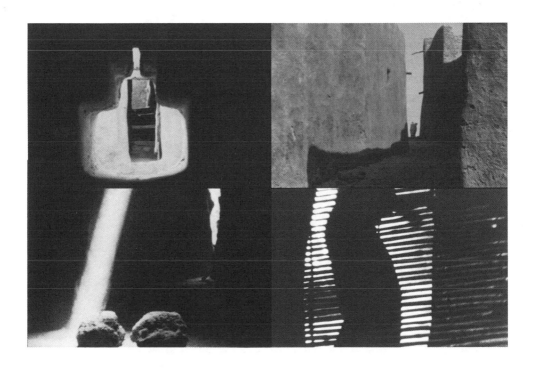

Mirrors multiplied and differently disposed . . . constituting a theater of illusions within which countless combinations of reflecting reflections operate. It is by virtue of consciousness of such a mirage-displacement that in Asian cultures the mirror often functions as the "symbol of the very void of symbols." . . . Writing is meshing one's writing with the machinery of endless reflexivity (Stills from **I-C**)

> I wonder why it should be so very difficult to be humble. . . . There seems to
> be some bad old pride in my heart; a root of it that puts out a thick shoot on
> the slightest provocation. . . . This interferes very much with work. One
> can't be calm, clear, good as one must be, while it goes on. . . . And anything
> that I write in this mood will be no good; it will be full of *sediment*. . . . One
> must learn, one must practise, to *forget* oneself. I can't tell the truth about
> Aunt Anne unless I am free to look into her life without self-consciousness.[34]

I read humble-*calm-clear*-good-truth versus old pride-interferes-*full of
sediment*-self-consciousness. And, for the time being, i retain: one *must*
learn to *forget oneself*. Are we dealing here with the old rule of objectivity
we have been taught in school in every composition class? Achieve distance, they keep on saying, as much distance from your own voice as
possible. Don't direct the reader's attention to yourself, don't fiddle with
words just to show off. For a woman, such a distance easily takes on the
face of Alienation. She must *learn* not only to impersonalize the voice she
stole or borrowed, but also to internalize gradually the impersonal generic
interpretation of masculine pronouns and nouns. She must *learn* to paint
her world with colors chosen more often than not by men for men to suit
their realities. *She-her* has always conveyed the idea of a personal and
gender-specific voice. In order to be taken more seriously, she is therefore
bound to dye this voice universal, a tint that can only be obtained through
words like *man, mankind, he-him.* The writer-he, the reader-he, the chair-
man, the cameraman, the protocolman. Such a convenient way to general-
ize and to transcend the sex line. One must practice to forget oneself, she
said. Again, as with the mirror relation, does this refer to the censorship of
a self-conscious (as opposed to self-effacing) voice so highly praised by
Good Writing as the means through which knowledge reaches abstraction
and is ideally freed from its existential roots? How estranged, deeply
estranged, she remains then. Silenced before she even finds the words to
name it. "Led into self-disdain by the great arm of parental-conjugal
phallocentrism" (as Hélène Cixous puts it). The good-equals-male type of
judgment is hard to kill even though it is avoided like the plague today for
its obsolescence. Margaret Atwood calls it "The Quiller-Couch Syndrome"
or "The Lady Painter Syndrome." The first name for it refers to an essay by
Quiller-Couch which defines the masculine and feminine types of writing
with adjectives like "objective" as opposed to "subjective" and "universal"
as opposed to "confessional," "personal," "narcissistic" and "neurotic."
The second refers to a statement by a male painter who artistic-ally post-
ulates: "When she's good, we call her a painter; when she's bad, we call
her a lady painter."[35] "Male" does not have to be present to exert its power.
She who writes well "writes like a man" and "thinks like a man"; that used
to be the highest praise a male reader could bestow upon a woman writer
or speaker (his wording may differ nowadays, but his criteria still often

grow from the same male-is-norm nutshell). What is implied here is her capability to write and think differently from other women who, wallowing in confessions and in personal, narcissistic, or neurotic accounts, are held to be hopelessly inept for either objective, subjective, or universal—that is to say accurate—thinking. Remember, the *minor*-ity's voice is always personal; that of the *major*-ity, always impersonal. Logic dictates. Man *thinks*, woman *feels*. The white man knows through *reason* and logic—the intelligible. The black man understands through *intuition* and sympathy—the sensible. Old stereotypes deriving from well-defined differences (the apartheid type of difference) govern our thought. Our province, we hear, is the *heart*, not the *mind*, which many of us have come to loathe and despise, for we believe it has a sex, a male one however, for reasons of (in)security. (We are told and we tell ourselves that we need to assert our identities.) But to write well, we must either espouse his cause or transcend our borderlines. We must forget ourselves. We are therefore triply jeopardized: as a writer, as a woman, and as a woman of color.

Writing woman

1) The Priest-God scheme (critique of relation of critic to work)
                                    critique of work as "work" as "product"

Writing in the feminine. And on a colored sky. How do you inscribe difference without bursting into a series of euphoric narcissistic accounts of yourself and your own kind? Without indulging in a marketable romanticism or in a naive whining about your condition? In other words, how do you forget without annihilating? Between the twin chasms of navel-gazing and navel-erasing, the ground is narrow and slippery. None of us can pride ourselves on being sure-footed there. Feminism can be iconoclastic, and all the more so when it calls itself Third World. But we have all let ourselves be infected with the leprosy of egotism, which remains the most difficult disease to cure, for what egotists, like lepers, inevitably undergo is a *loss of feeling* and are consequently apt to injure themselves without realizing it. I can let neither light nor air enter me when I close myself up and exist as a crystallized I, be this I feminine or masculine, female or male. Woman (with capital W) may therefore kill women if She loses the contact and speaks of Herself only according to what She wants to hear about Herself. A distinction needs to be made between "Write yourself. Write your body" and write about yourself, your body, your inner life, your fears, inhibitions, desires, and pleasures. The first refers to a scriptive act—the emergence of a writing-self—the second, to a consolidation of writing from the self. The two often overlap, but the type that consistently inundates the market is without doubt the second one: write-about biographies or novels, through whose stories the woman author constitutes an identity. A woman's room, despite its new seductive paneling, can become a prison as soon as it takes on the appearance of a lady's room (masculine notion of femininity) or a female's room (male's alter ego). The danger in going "the woman's way" is precisely that we may stop midway and limit ourselves to a series of reactions: instead of walking on, we are content with opposing woman('s emotion) to man('s abstraction), personal experience and anecdotes to impersonal invention and theory, in other words, with assuming the Quiller-Couch Syndrome. This is, obviously, not to say that the inner lives of women are of no interest nor that works dealing with women's feelings in a drawing room are less important than those dealing with war. No situation proves too small or too insignificant for a writer, since there is truly no narrow experience, only narrow representation. And narrow representation starts with the necessity of "I am God" or "I am Goddess" to create. The image of God alone making sky, earth, sea, and beings, transposed into writing, has led many of us to believe, as mentioned earlier, that the author exists *before* her/his own book, not simultaneously *with* it. The book perceived as an isolated materialization of something that precedes and exceeds it (the author's life, her/his thought or passion) is therefore bound to be a finished product, one whose content is expected to be entirely predetermined but whose form can always be ameliorated and further polished according to the ruling ideology of the "well written." Laying emphasis on the prestige of the individual and on the search for an explanation of the work in the wo/man who produces it (thereby perpetuating the myth of the original writer), literature remains completely dominated by the sovereignty of the author. On the one hand, the castrating objectivism of the "universal" writer; on the other hand, the obsessive personalism of the "singular" writer. Who is S/He? How does s/he create? How true, how authentic is her/his creation? How much of her/his real self has s/he inserted in her/his work? Writing, for the majority of us who call ourselves writers, still consists of "expressing" the exalted emotions related to the act of creating and either appropriating language to ourselves or ascribing it to a subject who is more or less a reflection of ourselves. The author's relation of antecedence, dependence, and possession to her/his work resembles that of a mother/father to her/his child. Like father, like son. Let us make man in our image, says the Bible. The writer is necessarily either God or Priest. As long as the belief in the sacred origin of writing and the religious principle of hidden meanings prevail, there will be a need for "veracious" interpretation and commentary. The Priest's role is to transcribe and/or explain as truthfully as possible God's confiding voice. The closer to this voice s/he claims to stand, the more weight her/his vision or opinion is likely to carry. Holy inspiration or faithful elucidation. Between critic and author, the relationship is the same as between author and God or author and imagination.

Here the formula reads: The task of criticism is to bring to light the enigmatic content of a work by reestablishing the ties between it and its author or reconstituting the latter's thought and experience through her/his works. God and Priest form an inseparable pair; the two often merge since the Priest represents God and rarely hesitates to assert her/his claims to God's *message*. Thus, no matter how novel her work may appear to be, the woman who writes about herself/others from the standpoint of the-one-who-knows deliberately/involuntarily carries on the conventions of the Priest-God scheme. Omniscient and omnipresent, she is everywhere and understands everything at the same time; she follows her own or her characters' outer expression and inner conscience simultaneously; she sees the present, past, and future of all events; and, above all, she has the power to dissolve the opacity of life. Eager to create a meaningful world and/or to unveil her ignored/censored deeper self, she adopts a series of strategies liable to ensure a transparency of form through which content, intelligibly constructed, can travel unhindered. Or she plays a hide-and-seek game with her readers, thus preserving the image of the mis-understood genius and leaving the task of guessing-rediscovering-clarifying to the critic. In many cases, she labors at confiding/confessing herself or at cutting herself sparingly into fragments and distributing them amongst her characters, with whom the readers may in their turn identify themselves. Charged with intentionality, writing is therefore disclosing (a secret), and reading is believing. The writer as a personified releaser of meaning produces envelopes whose more or less brilliant colors serve to decorate "the (theological) message." "Lost lady! Gentle fighter!" She sees God woman-shaped, because she reacts when she is told "And if they will learn anything let them ask their husbands at home: for it is a shame for women to speak in the church" (I Corinthians 14:35).

2) "And I grow younger as I leave my me behind"

The to-and-fro movement between the written woman and the writing woman is an endless one. "The woman took a train / away away from herself, . . . and I / grow younger as I leave / my me behind," Dilys Laing wrote, "They said: You took her with you / and brought her back again. / You look sick. Welcome home."[36] Yes, welcome home, for she has the impudence to disbelieve, to live before god. And after. She is "woman enough" to slip out of herself and go, then to return almost without self and without denying the going. Writing, in a way, is listening to the others' language and reading with the others' eyes. The more ears I am able to hear with, the farther I see the plurality of meaning and the less I lend myself to the illusion of a single message. I say I write when I leave

Writing: an ongoing practice concerned not with inserting a "me" into language, but with creating an opening where the "me" disappears while "I" endlessly come and go (Still from NS)

"I am a being of desire, therefore a being of words . . . who looks for her body and looks for the body of the other: for me, this is the whole history of writing" (Nicole Brossard) (Photos for **NS**)

Women's writings become nourricriture, a "linguistic flesh"
(Photos for **NS**)

(Photos for **NS**)

speech, when I lose my grip on it and let it make its way on its own. I am there only to provide it with a passageway. Why view these aspects of an individual which we imply in the term "writer" or "author" as projections of an isolated self and not of our common way of handling texts? For writing, like a game that defies its own rules, is an ongoing practice that may be said to be concerned, not with inserting a "me" into language, but with creating an opening where the "me" disappears while "I" endlessly come and go, as the nature of language requires. To confer an Author on a text is to close the writing. Eureka! It makes sense! *This is it!* I hold the key to the puzzle! Fear and seek. Fear and seek. The danger we fear most is forgetting to fear. Seek and lose. Lose, freely. When you are silent, it speaks; when you speak, it is silent. Writing is born when the writer is no longer. "In her own name she would have died of asphyxia. But once emerged from the membrane of self, spread out unto all the ways, coming to dwell at the brink of all sources." The greatest strength, Hélène Cixous further wrote, is "that of being no one, like a rose, of being pure joy before all naming. . . . How does the poet become self-strange to the point of the absolute innocence? Let herself be borne before thought, in thinking in preparation. . . . To become as simple as an apple, just like the goodness of an apple. . . . I am not ripe enough for innocence. Or yet too covered, too armed, too defended."[37] I am so much that nothing can enter me or pass through me. I struggle, I resist, and I am filled with my own self. The "personal" may liberate as it may enslave. We set it up against "impersonal" as if the two were mutually exclusive of each other, then start asserting that emphasis on the personal, the intimate, and the domestic has always been determining to the Women's Movement, hence the importance, for instance, of the personal diary form, which remains an effective means of self-expression for women to whom other avenues are often closed. True, but looking at the diary exclusively as a means of self-expression is already a distortion and a confinement. When I say I die when writing is or that I die to live, I am not referring to the opposition of life and death. We create the dualism, not realizing that death, like life, is a process. The moment I am born, I enter the realm of death. Life and death are together one process, and we are dying every moment. Writing so as not to die, we hear. Or so as to die? Every moment, I/i ask. To disarm death? Or to kill immortality? That composite, in-essential space where identity gives way to difference. She speaks about it as "images that shimmer around the edges," and she is lying low to let them develop. *She,* on the other hand, recalls it "as a voice fashioned out of shining darkness" and feels attracted toward "the tender light of an apple in the night." She insists: "It tells you. You don't tell it."—"The picture tells you how to arrange the words and the arrangement of the words tells you, or tells me, what's going on in the picture."[38] And *she* further specifies "their being glistened, came to pass, I came to pass, beside them, in humility."[39] Gleaming in the dark. Beware! This is it again, may be it. The Revelation, the Vision, the secret, the sacred origin of writing, that Holy Inspiration. *Not*-me should *not* hide or yield to a Higher Me, for the question involved is *not* that of obliterating the self for a purer truth—*non*-self, hence *no* self to die. Diana Chang wrote: "it wrote itself through me. I was driven and I drove the story onward. . . . Things I was not aware, I knew . . . it was her voice which started speaking through me. . . . I feel *she* wrote the novel. She knows what it means to have once been an actress, not I."[40] In her statement I read the anteriority of language to the writer. That which emerges from silence may be revealing, but it is revealing in the sense that language is always older than me. Never original, "me" grows indefinitely on ready-mades, which are themselves explainable only through other ready-mades. Spontaneity-personality in such a context does not guarantee more authenticity than stereotypy. Writing as an inconsequential process of sameness/otherness is ceaselessly re-breaking and re-weaving patterns of ready-mades. The written bears the written to infinity.

3) "Write your body"

It wrote itself through me. "Women must write through their bodies." Must not let themselves be driven away from their bodies. Must thoroughly rethink the body to re-appropriate femininity. Must not however exalt the body, not favor any of its parts formerly forbidden. Must perceive it in its integrity. Must and must-nots, their absolution and power. When armors and defense mechanisms are removed, when new awareness of life is brought into previously deadened areas of the body, women begin to experience writing/the world differently. This is exciting and also very scary. For it takes time to be able to tolerate greater aliveness. Hence the recurrence of musts and must-nots. As soon as a barrier is destroyed, another is immediately erected. Call it reform or expansion. Or else, well-defined liberation revolution. Closure and openness, again, are one ongoing process: we do not *have* bodies, we *are* our bodies, and we are ourselves while being the world. Who can endure constant open-endedness? Who can keep on living completely exposed? We write—think and feel—(with) our entire bodies rather than only (with) our minds or hearts. It is a perversion to consider thought the product of one specialized organ, the brain, and feeling, that of the heart. The past convention was that we desire because we are incomplete, that we are always searching for that other missing half. More recently, we no longer desire-because, we simply desire, and we desire as we are. "I am a being of desire, therefore a being of words," said Nicole Brossard, "a being who looks for her body and looks for the body of the other: for me, this is the whole history of writing."[41] Gathering the fragments of a divided, repressed body and reaching out to the other does not necessarily imply a lack or a deficiency. In writing themselves, women have attempted to render noisy and audible all that had been silenced in phallocentric discourse. "Your body must be heard," Hélène Cixous insists, "[Women] must invent the impregnable language that will wreck partitions, classes and rhetorics, regulations and codes."[42] Touch me and let me touch you, for the private is political. Language wavers with desire. It is "the language of my entrails," a skin with which I caress and feel the other, a body capable of receiving as well as giving: nurturing and procreating. Let it enter and let it go; writing myself into existence also means emptying myself of all that I can empty out—all that constitutes Old Spontaneous/Premeditated Me— without ceasing from being. "Every woman is the woman of all women" (Clarice Lispector). Taking in any voice that goes through me, I/i will answer every time someone says: I. One woman within another, eternally. "Writing as a woman. I am becoming more and more aware of this," notes Anaïs Nin, "All that happens in the real womb, not in the womb fabricated by man as a substitute. . . . woman's creation far from being like man's must be exactly like her creation of children, that is it must come out of her own blood, englobed by her womb, nourished by her own milk. It must be a human creation, of flesh, it must be different from man's abstractions."[43] Man is not content with referring to his creation as to his child, he is also keen on appropriating the life-giving act of childbearing. Images of men "in labor" and "giving birth" to poems, essays, and books abound in literature. Such an encroachment on women's domain has been considered natural, for the writer is said to be either genderless or bisexual. He is able to chat with both man's and woman's voices. This is how the womb is fabricated. Women began to be spoken of as if they were wombs on two feet when the fetus was described as a citizen, the womb was declared state property, legislation was passed to control it, and midwifery was kept under continual medical supervision—in other words, when women were denied the right to create. Or not to create. With their bodies. "All that happens in the real womb": writing as an "intrinsic" child/birth process takes on different qualities in women's contexts. No man claims to speak from the womb, women do. Their site of fertilization, they often insist, is the womb, not the mind. Their inner gestation is in the womb, not in the mind. The mind is therefore no longer opposed to the heart; it is, rather, perceived as part of the womb, being "englobed by it." Men name "womb" to separate a part of woman from woman (to separate it from the rest that forms her: body and mind), making it possible to lay legal claim to it. By doing so, they create their own contradictions and come round to identifying her with their fabrication: a specialized, infant-producing organ.

Women use "womb" to re-appropriate it and re-unite (or re-differ) them-selves, their bodies, their places of production. This may simply mean beating the master at his own game. But it may also mean asserting difference on differences. In the first case, the question is chiefly that of erecting inverted images and defying prohibitions. Annie Leclerc wrote:

> Let me first tell you where I get what I'm saying from, I get it from me, woman, and from my woman's belly. . . . Who would have told me, will I ever be able to tell, from what words shall I weave the bewildering happi-ness of pregnancy, the very rending, overwhelming happiness of giving birth. . . .
>
> So much the worst for him, I will have to speak of the joys of my sex, no, no, not the joys of my mind, virtue or feminine sensitivity, the joys of my woman's belly, my woman's vagina, my woman's breasts, sumptuous joys of which you have no idea at all.
>
> I will have to speak of them since it is only from them that a new, woman speech will be born.
>
> We will have to divulge what you have so relentlessly put in solitary confine-ment, for that is what all our other repressions build themselves upon.[44]

Woman's writing becomes "organic writing," "nurturing-writing" (nour-ricriture), resisting separation. It becomes a "connoting material," a "kneading dough," a "linguistic flesh." And it draws its corporeal fluidity from images of water—a water from the source, a deep, subterranean water that trickles in the womb, a meandering river, a flow of life, of words running over or slowly dripping down the pages. This keeping-alive and life-giving water exists simultaneously as the writer's ink, the mother's milk, the woman's blood and menstruation.[45] Logical backlash? An eye for an eye, a tooth for a tooth. Not quite, it seems. A woman's ink of blood for a man's ink of semen (an image found, for example, in Jacques Derrida's hymeneal fable: a sexual union in which the pen writes its in/dis/semination in the always folded/never single space of the hymen). In the second case—that of asserting difference on differences—the question of writing (as a) woman is brought a step further. Liquid/ocean associated with woman/mother is not just a facile play on words inherited from nineteenth-century Romantics (mer-mère in French). Motherhood as lived by woman often has little to do with motherhood as experienced by men. The mother cannot be reduced to the mother-hen, the wet-nurse, the year-round cook, the family maid, or the clutching, fear-inspiring matron. Mother of God, of all wo/mankind, she is role-free, non-Name, a force that refuses to be fragmented but suffocates codes (Cixous). In her maternal love, she is neither possessed nor possessive, neither binding nor detached nor neutral. For a life to maintain another life, the touch has to be infinitely delicate: precise, attentive, and swift, so as not to pull, track, rush, crush, or smother.[46] Bruised, half-alive, or dead is often the fate of what comes within the masculine grip. Woman, as Cixous defines her, is a whole—

"whole composed of parts that are wholes"—through which language is born over and over again. (The One is the All and the All is the One; and yet the One remains the One and the All the All. Not two, not One either. This is what Zen has been repeating for centuries.) To the classic conception of bisexuality, the self-effacing, merger-type of bisexuality, Cixous opposes "The *other bisexuality* . . . that is, each one's location in self *(repérage en soi)* of the presence—variously manifest and insistent according to each person, male or female—or both sexes, nonexclusion either of the difference or of one sex, and, from this 'self-permission,' multiplication of the effects of the inscription of desire, over all parts of my body and the other body."[47] The notion of "bisexual, hence neuter" writing together with the fantasy of a "total" being are concepts that many men have actively promoted to do away with differentiation. Androgyny is another name for such a co-optation. Saying that a great mind is androgynous (and *God knows* how many times we have heard this line—supposedly from Coleridge—and in how many disguises it appears) is equivalent to saying that "the mind has no sex" (also read "no gender"). In the salvation theme of androgyny, the male is still seen as the active power of generation and the female as the passive one (a defective male, due to the absence of androgen). Thus Janice Raymond suggests as a substitute the word "integrity"; she expands it and redefines it as "an unfolding process of becoming. It contains within itself an insatiable generativeness, that is, a compulsion to reproduce itself in every diverse fashion."[48] In every diverse fashion . . . Laying claim to the specificity of women's sexuality and the rights pertaining to it is a step we have to go through in order to make ourselves heard; in order to beat the master at his own game. But reducing everything to the order of sex does not, obviously, allow us to depart from a discourse directed within the apparatuses of sexuality. Writing does not translate bisexuality. It (does not express language but) fares across it.

4) The body in theory

It must be different from man's abstractions. Different from man's androgenization. Man's fragmentization. Ego is an identification with the mind. When ego develops, the head takes over and exerts a tyrannical control over the rest of the body. (The world created must be defended against foreign infiltration.) But thought is as much a product of the eye, the finger, or the foot as it is of the brain. If it is a question of fragmenting so as to decentralize instead of dividing so as to conquer, then what is needed is perhaps not a clean erasure but rather a constant displacement of the two-by-two system of division to which analytical thinking is often subjected. In many cases emphasis is necessarily placed upon a reversal of the hierarchy implied in the opposition between mind and body, spiritual and material, thinking and feeling, abstract and concrete, theory and practice. However, to prevent this counter-stance from freezing into a dogma (in which the dominance-submission patterns remain unchanged), the strategy of mere reversal needs to be displaced further, that is to say, neither simply renounced nor accepted as an end in itself. In spite of the distant association, one example that comes to mind are the procedures which in Asia postulate not one, not two, but three centers in the human being: the intellectual (the *path*), the emotional (the *oth*), and the vital (the *kath*). The martial arts concentrate on developing awareness of the latter, which they call the *tantien* or the *hara*. This center, located below the navel (the oth being connected with the heart, and the path with reason), radiates life. It directs vital movement and allows one to relate to the world with instinctual immediacy. But instinct(ual immediacy) here is not opposed to reason, for it lies outside the classical realm of duality assigned to the sensible and the intelligible. So does certain women's womb writing, which neither separates the body from the mind nor sets the latter against the heart (an attitude which would lead us back to the writing-as-birth-delivering-labor concept and to the biologico-metaphorization of women's bodies previously discussed) but allows each part of the body to become infused with consciousness. Again, bring a new awareness of life into previously forgotten, silenced, or deadened areas of the body. Consciousness here is not the result of an accumulation of knowledge and experience but the term of an ongoing unsettling process. The formula "Know thyself" has become obsolete. We don't want to observe our organism from a safe distance. We do not just write about our body, whether in a demonstrative (objectivist) or a submissive (subjectivist) discourse. Knowledge leads no more to openings than to closures. The idealized quest for knowledge and power makes it often difficult to admit that enlightenment (as exemplified by the West) often brings about endarkenment. More light, less darkness. More darkness, less light. It is a question of degrees, and these are two degrees of one phenomenon. By attempting to *exclude* one (darkness) for the sake of the other (light), the modernist project of building universal knowledge has indulged itself in such self-gratifying oppositions as civilization/ primitivism, progress/backwardness, evolution/stagnation. With the decline of the colonial idea of advancement in rationality and liberty, what becomes more obvious is the necessity to reactivate that very part of the modernist project at its *nascent* stage: the radical calling into question, in every undertaking, of everything that one tends to take for granted—which is a (pre- and post-modernist) stage that should remain constant. No Authority no Order can be safe from criticism. Between knowledge and power, there is room for knowledge-without-power. Or knowledge at rest—"the end of myths, the erosion of utopia, the rigor of taut patience,"[49] as Maurice Blanchot puts it. The terrain remains fresh for it cannot be occupied, not even by its specific creator. The questions that arise continue to provoke answers, but none will dominate as long as the ground-clearing activity is at work. Can knowledge circulate without a position of mastery? Can it be conveyed without the exercise of power? No, because there is no end to understanding power relations which are rooted deep in the social nexus—not merely added to society nor easily locatable so that we can just radically do away with them. Yes, however, because in-between grounds always exist, and cracks and interstices are like gaps of fresh air that keep on being suppressed because they tend to render more visible the failures operating in every system. Perhaps mastery need not coincide with power. Then we would have to rethink mastery in terms of non-master, and we would have to rewrite women's relation to theory. "Writing the body" may be immediately heard by a number of male or genderless writers as "imitating" or "duplicating the body." It may be further read as "female self-aggrandizement" or "female neurosis." (It falls on deaf ears, most likely . . .) *There is no such thing as a direct relation to the body,* they assert. For them writing the body means writing *closer* to the body, which is understood as being able to express itself directly without any social mediation. The biological remains here conveniently separate from the sociohistorical, and the question "where does the social stop in the biological?" and vice versa, is not dealt with. They read "writing the body" as "the (biological) body writing itself." They either can't hear the difference or believe there is only *one way* of hearing it: the way they define it. Putting an end to further explorations they often react with anger: *that's not deep enough! What is it supposed to mean?* If we take the case of Roland Barthes, who also passionately writes the (impetus of the) body, the question of depth and meaning no longer exerts its tyranny: he might be fetishist, some of them admit, but We love his fetishism; it's *intelligently* written! and theoretically sound! Through the works of a number of male writers, "writing the body" may be accepted as a concept because attempts at theorizing it have been carried out, and it has its own place as theoretical object. But when this concept-practice is materialized, the chance of its being understood or even recognized as such never goes without struggle. On the one hand it is a commonplace to say that "theoretical" usually refers to inaccessible texts that are addressed to a privileged, predominantly male social group. Hence, to many men's ears it is synonymous with "profound," "serious," "substantial," "scientific," "consequential," "thoughtful," or "thought-engaging"; and to many women's ears, equivalent to "masculine," "hermetic," "elitist," and "specialized," therefore "neutral," "impersonal," "purely mental," "unfeeling," "disengaging," and—last but not least—"abstract." On the other hand, it is equally common to observe that theory threatens, for it can upset rooted ideologies by exposing the mechanics of their workings. It shakes established canons and questions every norm validated as "natural" or "human." And it undermines a powerful tradition of "aesthetics" and "scholarship" in the liberal arts, in the humanities as well as in the social sciences. To say this is also to say that theory is suspicious, as long as it remains an occupied territory. Indeed, theory no longer is theoretical when it loses sight of its own conditional nature, takes no risk in speculation, and circulates as a form of administrative inquisition. Theory oppresses, when it wills or perpetuates existing power relations, when it presents itself as a means to exert authority—the Voice of Knowledge. In the passage from the heard, seen, smelled, tasted, and touched to the told and the written, language has taken place. Yet in the articulation of language, what is referred to, phenomenally and philosophically, is no more important than what is at work, linguistically, in the referring activity. To declare, for example, that so-and-so is an authority on such-and-such matter (implying thereby that s/he has written with authority on the subject concerned and that this authority is recognized by his/her peers) is to lose sight of the radicalness of writing and theorizing. It is to confuse the materiality of the thing named—or the object of discussion—with the materiality of the name—the modalities of production and reception of meaning—and to give up all attempt at understanding the very social and historical reality of the tools one uses to unmask ideological mystifications—including the mystification of theory. What is at stake is not so much the referential function of language as the authority of language as a model for natural cognition and a transparent medium for criticizing and theorizing. The battle continues, as it should, on several fronts. If it is quite current today to state that language functions according to principles that are not necessarily (like) those of the phenomenal world, it is still unusual to encounter instances where theory involved the voiding, rather than the affirming or even reiterating, of theoretical categories. Instances where poeticalness is not primarily an aesthetic response, nor literariness merely a question of pure verbalism. And instances where the borderline between theoretical and non-theoretical writings is blurred and questioned, so that theory and poetry necessarily mesh, both determined by an awareness of the sign and the destabilization of the meaning and writing subject. To be lost, to encounter impasse, to fall, and to desire both fall and impasse—isn't this what happens to the body in theory? For, in theorizing, can women afford to forget, as Marguerite Duras puts it, that "men are the ones who started to speak, to speak alone and for everyone else, on behalf of everyone else. . . . They activated the old language, enlisted the aid of the old way of theorizing, in order to relate, to recount, to explain this new situation"?[50] Indeed, women rarely count among those whom Catherine Clément describes as being "greedy of the slightest theoretical breaking of wind that is formulated, eager not to miss any coach of a passing train in which they hop in flocks behind their chief, whoever he may be, provided that they are not alone and that it is a question of things of the mind."[51] Difference needs not be suppressed in the name of Theory. And theory as a tool of survival needs to be rethought in relation to gender in discursive practice. Generally speaking, it is not difficult to agree with Duras that "men don't translate. They begin from a theoretical platform that is already in place, already elaborated. [Whereas] The writing of women is really translated from the unknown, like a new way of communicating rather than an already formed language. But to achieve that, we have to turn away from plagiarism." More specifically speaking, however, it is difficult to be content with statements she puts forth such as: "Reverse everything. Make women the point of departure in judging, make darkness the point of departure in judging what men call light, make obscurity the point of departure in judging what men call clarity. . . ."[52] Unless "point of departure" is constantly re-emphasized so that, again, reversal strategies do not become end points in themselves. Language defying language has to find its own place, in which claiming the right to language and disqualifying this same right work together without leading to the mystical, much-indulged-in angst that pervades many men's works. By its necessary tautness, writing the body in theory sometimes chokes to the breaking point. But the break, like the fall and impasse mentioned earlier, is desired. I do not write simply to destroy, conserve, or transmit. To re-appropriate a few sentences of Blanchot's, I write in the thrall of the impossible (feminine ethnic) real, that share of the detour of inscription which is always a de-scription.[53] From jagged transitions between the analytical and the poetical to the disruptive, always shifting fluidity of a headless and bottomless storytelling, what is exposed in this text is the inscription and de-scription of a non-unitary female subject of color through her engagement, therefore also disengagement, with master discourses. Mastery ensures the transmission of knowledge; the dominant discourse for transmitting is one "that annihilates sexual difference—where there is no question of it." "Her discourse, even when 'theoretical' or political, is never simple or linear or 'objectivized,' universalized; she involves her story in history" (Cixous).[54] Like Monique Wittig's and Sande Zeig's bearers of fables, women "are constantly moving, they recount, among other things, the metamorphosis of words from one place to another. *They* themselves *change* versions of these metamorphoses, *not in order to further confuse the matter but because they record the changes.* The result of these changes is an avoidance of fixed meanings. . . . They agree upon the words that they do not want to forgo. Then they decide, according to their groups, communities, islands, continents, on the possible tribute to be paid for the words. When that is decided, they pay it (or they do not pay it). Those who do so call this pleasantly 'to write one's life with one's blood,' this, they say, is the least they can do."[55] "Writing the body" is that abstract-concrete, personal-political realm of excess not fully contained by writing's unifying structural forces. Its physicality (vocality, tactility, touch, resonance), or edging and margin, exceeds the rationalized "clarity" of communicative structures and cannot be fully explained by any analysis. It is a way of making theory in gender, of making of theory a politics of everyday life, thereby re-writing the ethnic female subject as site of differences. It is on such a site and in such a context that resistance to theory yields more than one reading. It may be a mere form of anti-intellectualism—a dis-ease that dwells on the totalizing concept of theory and practice and partakes in the Master's norms of clarity and accessibility while perpetuating the myth of the elite versus the mass, of those who think versus those who do not think. It may also be a distrust of the use of language about language and could be viewed in terms of both resistance and attraction to language itself. For to say that language is caught within a culturally and sexually dominent ideology is not to deny the heterogeneous history of its formation or, in other words, to refuse to "see race, class *and* gender determinations in the formation of language" (Gayatri C. Spivak).[56] Woman as subject can only redefine while being defined by language. Whatever the position taken ("no position" is also a position, for "I am not political" is a way of accepting "my politics is someone else's"), the love-hate, inside-outside, subject-of-subject-to relation between woman and language is inevitably always at work. That holds true in every case—whether she assumes language is a given, hence the task of the writer is merely to build vocabularies and choose among the existing possibilities; whether she decides to "steal" demonstrative and discursive discourse from men (Clément), since language cannot free itself from the male-is-norm ideology and its subsuming masculine terms; whether she asserts that language is primarily a tool for transmitting knowledge, therefore there is no attributable difference between masculine and feminine writing and no shift needs to be made (in language and) in metalanguage, whose repressive operations "see to it that the moment women open their mouths—women more often than men—they are immediately asked in whose name and from what theoretical standpoint they are speaking, who is their master and where they are coming from: they have, in short, to salute . . . and show their identity papers";[57] whether she affirms that language is heterogeneous, claims her right to it, and feels no qualms in reproducing existing power relations because she has discoursed on this issue; or whether she insists that the production of woman-texts is not possible without a writing that inscribes "femininity," just as writing woman cannot address the question of difference and change (it cannot be a political reflection) without reflecting and working on language.

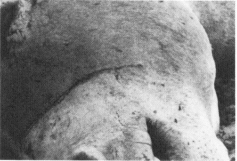

"They only speak their own language and when they hear other sounds—no language to their ear—they walk off warily, affirming: "It's not deep enough, we haven't learnt anything" (Stills from **R**)

II.

The Language of Nativism: Anthropology as a Scientific Conversation of Man with Man

*faculty once asked me, "why are you in Anthopology?"
I replied, "because its so much easier to love all of Mankind
    than one solitary man"*

—Barbara San Severina, "A Grass Model" in *Stalking
    the Evil That's Been Giving Darkness a Bad Name*

*That the birds of
Worry and care
Fly about your
Head, this you
Cannot change,
But that they build
Nests in your hair,
This you can prevent*

—Chinese proverb

The reign of worn codes

In sight of every reader-by, let him run naked. Here, where she lives, each door revolves like a mirror of his mirror, and repression takes on the forms of both suppressed and forced speech. If she does not ravel and unravel his universe, she will then remain silent, looking at him looking at her. Or she will, with the enthusiasm of the blind leading the blind, walk in his footsteps chanting R-adical-evolution. He belongs to that fraction of humanity which for centuries has made other fractions the objects of contempt and exploitation, then, when it saw the handwriting on the wall, set about to give them back their humanity. In view of such eternal recuperation, she can no longer align any trace on the page without at the same time recognizing the trace of his traces. Drifting from one (shore) to another, she therefore steps into his universe, wavering between the will to release and the desire to hold back. Sometimes she takes pleasure in wearing shoes three sizes bigger than her feet and coats so large as to turn herself to a mere hanger. Other times she realizes she is the proverbial toad striving for the impressive capaciousness of the cow and puffing itself up to the point of bursting. We set out here, she and I, to undo an *anonymous*, all-male, and predominantly white collective entity named *he*, and we wish to freeze him once in a while in his hegemonic variants. Knowledge requires a certain dialectic of information and control, and I think it may help to reverse our roles once in a while, more for the emergence of a certain awareness than for the gratification of aping. I have wondered time and again about my reading myself as I feel he reads me and my false encounter with the other in me whose non-being/being he claims to have captured, solidified, and pinned to a butterfly board. Like any common living thing, I fear and reprove classification and the death it entails, and I will not allow its clutches to lock down on me, although I realize I can never lure myself into simply escaping it. The difference, as I sense it, is: naming, like a cast of the die, is just one step toward unnaming, a tool to render visible what he has carefully kept invisible in his manipulative blindness. I never really start or end the trial process; I persist. Constantly changing my point of departure or arrival, I trace, void, retrace with the desire to baffle rather than bring out contours. Some lines, some curves may emerge, whose totality will always differ. The further I persevere, the more liable I am to let myself be riddled by doubts. On one plane, we, I and he, may speak the same language and even act alike; yet, on the other, we stand miles apart, irreducibly foreign to each other. This is partly due to our distinct actualities and our definite history of involvement and power relationship. What I resent most, however, is not his inheritance of a power he so often disclaims, disengaging himself from a system he carries with him, but his ear, eye, and pen, which record in his language while pretending to speak through mine, on my behalf. I thereby do not oppose to eliminate. I'd rather make of writing a site where opposites lose their essential differences and are restored to the void by their own in-terchangeability. Thus, I see no interest in adopting a progression that systematically proceeds from generalities to specificities, from outlines to fillings, from diachronic to synchronic, or vice versa. And I am profoundly indifferent to his old way of theorizing—of piercing, as he often claims, through the sediments of psychological and epistemological "depths." I may stubbornly turn around a foreign thing or turn it around to play with it, but I respect its realms of opaqueness. Seeking to perforate meaning by forcing my entry or breaking it open to dissipate what is thought to be its secrets seems to me as crippled an act as verifying the sex of an unborn child by ripping open the mother's womb. It is typical of a mentality that proves incapable of touching the living thing without crushing its delicateness. I undeniably prefer the heterogeneity of free play in a dice game to the unity and uniformity of dissection, classification, and synthesis toward a higher truth. It is with and within the reign of worn codes or, perhaps more precisely, here within the boundaries of what he says he is or does that I intend to play and spin. I am temporarily referring to him in the third person, the pronoun of the non-person, since he claims to be the spokesman for the entire human race—never hesitating to speak about and for a vague entity named *man* whose putative universality no longer fools anyone. I will further delete all proper names and use representative stereotyped appellations to refer to the famed individuals of his objectively impersonal world. Omnipresent even in his absent being, he has invaded the homes of the wise and left his rottenness in every piece of land he set foot on. I shall never catch enough of him, for my human language-net excludes totalization, and my gesture is a continuation striving for continuation. One of the rules of my game is to echo back his words to an unexpected din or simply let them bounce around to yield most of what is being and has been said through them and despite them. I am therefore not concerned with judging the veracity of his discourse in relation to some original truth—a veracity he always implies through his scientism, professionalism, or "scholarism." Perhaps by dint of persisting in this net play, I shall succeed in reproducing a few traits of the numbness of a tradition which he happily spreads about, often "without his being aware of it." Perhaps also, I shall succeed in exposing some of the premises of oppression and hegemony I and you often accept into our discourse the very moment we apply ourselves to denouncing them. (By hegemony, I am referring to the authority of certain states over others, of one sex over the other, and to the form of cultural and sexual ascendency that once worked through direct domination but now often operates via consent—hence its pernicious, long-lasting, and binding strength.) I thus thread my way into the snares of his universe, borrowing this first observation: "All that the action of love obtains from me is merely this wisdom: that the other is not to be known; [her or] his opacity is not the screen around a secret, but, instead, a kind of evidence in which the game of reality and appearance is done away with."[1]

The positivist dream: We, the natives; They, the natives

The story of man's infatuation with his language is an unending one. In a remote village of Africa, a wise Dogon man used to say "to be naked is to

I shall never catch enough of him, for my human language-net excludes totalization, and my gesture is a continuation striving for continuation (Stills from **I-C**)

be speechless."[2] Power, as unveiled by numerous contemporary writings, has always inscribed itself in language. Speaking, writing, and discoursing are not mere acts of communication; they are above all acts of compulsion. Please follow me. Trust me, for deep feeling and understanding require total commitment. In the global village, what concerns me concerns you. The attempt to impose a human reality onto an inexplicably indifferent world is as obvious, as tangible as language can be in its crude being. A thoughtful white man observed not long ago that "there is no reality not already classified by men: to be born is nothing but to find this code ready-made and to be obligated to accommodate oneself to it."[3] Power therefore never dies out: tracked, pursued, wornout, or driven away here, it will always reappear there, where I expect it least. And language is one of the most complex forms of subjugation, being at the same time the locus of power and unconscious servility. With each sign that gives language its shape lies a stereotype of which I/i am both the manipulator and the manipulated. Transposed onto another plane, such is the relation, for example, between we, the natives, and they, the natives. From a voluntary to an enforced designation, the distance is plain but the appearance remains intentionally ambiguous. Terming us the "natives" focuses on *our* innate qualities and our belonging to a particular place by birth; terming them the "natives," on *their* being born inferior and "non-Europeans." As homonyms, these two "natives" sometimes claim to merge and other times hear nothing of each other. The further I disentangle social anthropology, the deeper I entangle myself. Where is that ethnic me? the Other? The more I accept his word-prescriptions, the more my *competences* shrink. From "forget who you are and forget me not" to "know who you are and copy me not," the point of view is the same: "Be like *us.*" The goal pursued is the spread of a hegemonic dis-ease. Don't be us, this self-explanatory motto warns. Just be "like" and bear the chameleon's fate, never infecting *us* but only yourself, spending your days muting, putting on/taking off glasses, trying to please all and always at odds with myself who is no self at all. Yet, being accused of "ignoring one's own culture" and "looking whiter than Snow White herself" also means taking a trip to the promised land of White Alienation. The language in which *I perceive* (quite a deception) myself—cultur-ally, psychologic-ally, physic-ally, and spiritu-ally (What hasn't he contaminated? Can you name it?)—and become aware of my *needs* is permeated with professional definitions. *Anthropo Logical Hegemony*, a non-universal homocentrism that brings in light where obscurity reigns. I name the way he names, aspire to the same freedom he cherishes, and look carefully at my "roots," not venturing to speak about any single (my) traditional society without his advice, the expert anthropologist's. Has anything changed since "indigenous" took over, rendering "native" obsolete? Whatever the answer, if you want to avoid sounding like an old(-fashioned) racist, a colonist, a backward SETTLER, be sure never to talk about manifestations of "primitive religion": "devil-worship," "fetish-ism," "animism," and the like are a no-(liberal)-man's-land. Remember, "traditional religions"—yes, "religion" is the "right" expression—for that is how equality is distributed, given, or gained.

"Religion" institutionalized is a purely Western concept; a learned white man has demonstrated as much. You know it, don't you, who have directly or indirectly written accounts of *The Nature of the Non-Western World, How Natives Think*, and *The "Soul" of the Primitive*. Of *The Savage Mind* and *The Sexual Life of Savages*. Of *Primitive Mentality* and *The Making of Religion*. Then, of "Asian Westernism" and "African Philosophies." Striving for the Other's mind and redefining the intangible is "human." You can no doubt capture, tame, and appropriate it to yourself, for language as a form of knowing will always provide you with Your other. One of the conceits of anthropology lies in its positivist dream of a neutralized language that strips off all its singularity to become nature's exact, unmisted reflection. The perfect double excludes difference and is neither one nor exactly two. What he means and means well, between the lines, is the Same and the Other. What is perceived, however, through his language and despite it, is either the Same and the Same, or the Same versus the Other. Again, be like *us*, a collective identification that includes or excludes me with an identical passion. How can I not be like you? Some struggle to stand out from the crowd, others find happiness in standing with the crowd. Crowd reads opaque, it may become mob, crush, rout, and horde. Not his language, which he wishes to render transparent, believing he could erase himself in his writing while clinging to the *author's* mastership. The claim to objectivity subjects words to a willed meaning-intention. Do I make sense? Meaningful language is confined to "expression" and what appears significant to him is its reduction to pure instrumentality: a minimum presence and yet an effective defensive weapon. Words are solicited only for their effacement from the page. Their materiality, their glaring bodies must somehow sink and disappear from the field of visibility, to yield ground to the "pure presence" or that which he attempts to capture and retain, which, however, always lies outside of words.

Words have no power, truly. They, like a Zen master's definition of "Buddha," are no more than "dried dung"; with it you and I hold our preaching house together. Wet dung remains an environmental potential. In many societies it serves to plaster earthen walls, protecting them from the weather. This is the way the West carries the burden of the Other. Naming is part of the human rituals of incorporation, and the unnamed remains less human than the inhuman or sub-human. The threatening Otherness must, therefore, be transformed into figures that belong to a definite image-repertoire. According to the same learned white man, the concept that is currently termed "development" has gone through six stages of metamorphosis since late antiquity. The perception of the outsider as the one who needs help has taken on the successive forms of the barbarian, the pagan, the infidel, the wild man, the "native," and the underdeveloped.[4] Needless to say, these forms whose meanings helplessly keep on decomposing can only exist in relation to their opposites. "The barbarian is, in the first place, the man who believes in barbarism."[5] The setting up of unitary opposites is a result of the well-meant intention of equating the unequal, which thereby assumes its responsibility for the constraints of equality while allowing inequality to maintain its being. Thus, the invention of "needs" and the mission to "help" the needy always blossom together. The Full Man, the Church, the Humanist, the Civilized-Colonist, and the Professional-Anthropologist all have a human face and are close male agnates descending from the same key ancestor. Writing about the spread of the White Cancer, an endangering attitude of mind whose response to the Others varies only according to the manner in which it believes the Others could be rescued from their situation, an Indian man remarks:

> The white man is problem-solving. His conceptualizations merge into science and then emerge in his social life as problems, the solution of which are the adjustments of his social machine.

As an abstract, dominant non-group, whites have always been tempted to define groups in their most superficial aspects,

> Hence, we have white, black, red, and the Yellow Peril. And we are taught to speak of the *Negro problem*, the *Indian problem*. . . . A man is defined as a white, Anglo-Saxon Protestant, healthy, ambitious, earnest, and honest, a man whom the Lord smiles upon by increasing the fruits of his labor. Welfare is designed to compensate people insofar as they deviate from that norm. . . . Welfare buys that portion of a person which does not match the stereotype of the real man.[6]

To measure the extent of the White Cancer action is to recognize how much you and I have let *that portion of ourselves which does not match the stereotype of the real man* be consumed in our very determination to preserve it.

Anthropology is defined as a science of *man* or "a *study* of the *nature* of the *human* s-p-e-c-i-e-s." Next to the mind doctors—the psychiatrist, psychoanalyst, and psychologist—is the anthropologist, who also pretends to the precision of a zoologist or a botanist. As purveyor of "truth," he has moved from the absolute to the relative and now assumes the role of purveyor of "certain truths," pursuing a "perspectivistic knowledge" while keeping an eye profoundly glued on "scientific objectivity" as methodological goal. Some indignantly deny the presence of object in objectivity and say of those who read in this term a tendency to turn people into odd insects for investigation that they are suffering from "a lack of epistemological knowledge." Insects move, things don't. Consequently, objectivity preserved as an ability to surpass (or bypass) the obstacles of oneself should be distinguished from "realism," which "consists in ignoring the existence of oneself and [therefore] taking one's own view for immediately objective and absolute."[7] Besides the insect factor, don't forget that identifying with the needy alien from the subordinate cultural system will most likely yield negative results. The *proper* anthropologist should be prevented from "going over the hill," should be trained for detachment in the field if he wishes to remain on the winning side. The classic example of the man who spent years trying to learn the religious secrets of a particular society and refused to divulge them once he became a member of that cult has been seen as a *loss*, a loss of objectivity, for the man changed sides and—why not say it?—betrayed his own kind, the kind of his "origins." It never appeared as a gain such that this man simply decided to opt for a different scale of values, a different way of living. Equal alternative happy ending. "Why bother to get married?" says a man, "I want to remain myself. Once you get too involved, it can never be the same again!" Excerpt from our ordinary musical environment followed by an episode of language that stages the loss of the true self: here, he runs counter to the law of being; the fear of a one-way assimilation can only resolve into its active materialization (I do not believe in marriage because I cannot view relationship with the Other except as a yielding of presence-power). It reflects, under a new light, the same positivist dream of a perfect double, and reduces the weaving of two or several family webs to nothing else but: the Burden of the Other.

A Western Science of man

Anthropology reified as the study of man which never comes close to a general definition of man by identifying in him a single quality that is at the same time specific, irreducible, and universal. The purveyor of Truth or certain anthropomorphic truths can equally be called the purveyor of Error or certain anthropomorphic errors. On the watch for the uncontaminated aspects of a culture, whose marrow is believed to lie hidden somewhere behind the "fundamental" beliefs, ideology, and behavior of its members, our anthropologist "has not only to spread his nets in the right place, and wait for what will fall into them. He must be an active huntsman, and drive his quarry into them and follow it up to its most inaccessible lairs." These are indeed "the more active methods of pursuing [anthropological] evidence."[8] Have you ever attended a white man's presentation (often also ours) on a "native" society, be he a photographer, a filmmaker, a choreographer, a musician, a speaker, or a writer? It is as if, unvaryingly, every single look, gesture, or utterance has been stained with anthropological discourse, the only discourse in power when it is a question of the (native) Other. Knowledge belongs to the one who succeeds in mastering a language, and standing closer to the civilized language is, as a matter of fact, coming nearer to equality. "In popular thinking, we imagine that the natives live on the bosom of Nature, more or less as they can and like, the prey of irregular, phantasmagoric beliefs and apprehensions. Modern science, on the contrary, shows that their social institutions have a very definite organization." The anthropologist is one of those rare creatures who devotes his time to working for the losing side. He "has introduced law and order into what seemed chaotic and freakish. [He] has transformed for us the sensational, wild and unaccountable world of 'savages' into a number of well-ordered communities governed by law, behaving and thinking according to consistent principles."[9] Any investigator who claims to be merely "recording facts" thereby deludes himself, for the Great Master has said it: "*Only laws and generalizations are scientific facts,* and field work consists only and exclusively in the preparation of the chaotic reality, in subordinating it to general rules."[10] "Discourse," "law," "order," "generalizations," "consistency"—what he values and looks for is, fortunately, what he always only finds.

Anthropology as a Western science of man studies man as *the* human species. He who *knows* how to distinguish the *real* from the *false,* investigates man and woman indifferently as male and female "social animals." "Collecting concrete data of evidence and drawing the general inferences for [the anthropologist] himself . . . was not found out or at least practised in Ethnography till field work was taken up by men of sciences."[11] Thus, the first step the scientific investigator ought to take is to observe the skin of native life and record it undifferentiatingly in its minute details. This "method of concrete, statistical documentation" has been recognized as the means through which he traces the *anatomy* of a culture. What remains for the next steps, as you may already have guessed, is the flesh and the bone. These are the study of acts of tribal life such as ceremonies, rites, and festivities called "the imponderabilia of actual life and of typical behavior" and the collection of statements, narratives, items of folklore, and magical formulae considered as a *"corpus inscriptionum,* as documents of native mentality."[12] The Great Master has decreed that:

> The *scientific* treatment differs from that of good common sense, first in that a student will extend the completeness and minuteness of survey much further and in a pedantically systematic and methodical manner; and secondly, in that the scientifically trained mind, will push the inquiry along really relevant lines, and towards aims possessing real importance.

"Complete," "systematic," "methodical," "scientifically trained," "really relevant," "aims," "real importance"—so much of the scientific mind condensed in such a repetitively short statement. Common sense turns out to be the kingdom of the mute, the unreal, and the "illiterate."

> The time when we could tolerate accounts presenting us the native as a distorted, childish caricature of a human being is gone. This picture is false, and like many other falsehoods, it has been killed by Science.[13]

Who gave out such accounts and who hastened to correct them? Who discredited them as shameful lies and set off to discover the truth? The Great Master has made it clear: anthropology is a question of paying off old scores between white men. Science is Truth, and what anthropology seeks first and foremost through its noble defense of the native's cause (whose cause? you may ask) is its own elevation to the rank of Science. Sharing the Great Master's endeavor, men highly committed to their academic community continue thus to maintain that "anthropology is not the bastard of colonialism but the legitimate offspring of the Enlightenment" and suggest with complacency that "despite their failings, social anthropologists have on the whole been at least as competent and perceptive as *factory inspectors* . . . and perhaps have worked harder and suffered more" (my italics).[14] The anthopologist's task of verifying, challenging(?), and readjusting the scientific activity of *a certain society*—his own—comes well before that of promoting communication between peoples of different "cultures" (one more task open to discussion). Anthropology as human science is nowadays the foundation of every single discourse pronounced above the native's head. It is, as an African man observed, "the diary of the white man in mission; the white man commissioned by the historical sovereignty of European thinking and its peculiar vision of man."[15] What has been written never addresses the Yellow, the Black, or the Red. The anthropologist's pen smudges are by-products of a science of man in which the non-civilized man—the very element that permitted its founding—is excluded. Preconceived ideas, as the Great Master has proclaimed, are pernicious in any scientific work, but scientific logic has unhesitatingly allowed anthropology to speak about (some) men in terms such as man and human. What a man looks for, as already mentioned, is fortunately what he always/never finds: a perfect reflection of himself.

> Perhaps as *we* read the account of these remote customs there may emerge a feeling of solidarity with the endeavours and ambitions of *these natives*. Perhaps *man's* mentality will be revealed to *us*, and brought near, along some lines which we never have followed before. Perhaps through realising *human* nature in a shape very distant and foreign to us, we shall have some light shed on *our* own. In this, and in this case only, we shall be justified in feeling that it has been worth *our* while to understand these natives, *their* institutions and customs. . . .[16] (my italics)

Anthropology revalidated with a sham cynicism as "the study of men in crisis by men in crisis." A cynicism that inadvertently and unavoidably points back to the positivist dream. Language also reveals its power through an insignificant slip of the pen, for no matter how one tries to subject it to control and reduce it to "pure" instrumentality, it always succeeds in giving an inkling of its irreducible governing status. The anthropologist has come to see the illusion of treating "the indigene as an object" and now claims to be himself an "object of contemporary, imperial civilization." He who defines his situation as "the quintessence of alienation" and explains it as a "split between the person and the professional" considers himself to be a victim. He courageously assumes the "entropologist's" fate and lets himself be "estranged three times over: first, in his own society, along with the generality of his fellow citizens; secondly, in the choice of his profession; and finally, in relation to those he studies." In his *professionalism*, the anthropologist is said to be an alien who "claims the whole of the Western tradition for his ancestry" and by "claiming everything . . . is in danger of being nothing."[17] Thus, colonizer and colonized have come to speak the same language. Don't complain of being alienated, for it is *We* who undergo the "true," quintessential alienation, *We* whose faith in our profession robs us of our *being* and reduces us into a *being nothing*. The vicious cycle continues its course. The Powerless have learned to parrot the language of the Powerful. It all depends on where you stand and on which side the scale is weighted. One truth at home and another abroad. The same logic compels the native to endure the enculturation process and resist acculturation. Caught in an unresolvable contradiction,

the anthropologist now sees a need to "train Third World anthropologists," for "*Comprador* intellectuals of the Third World are hardly
less likely to be racism-free or anticolonial . . . than outsiders." Often
displaying "a depressing elitism," many of them are said to exclude anthropologists from their nations "through fear of accurate social analyses of
the new sorts of discrimination."[18] This is true in many ways, for we have
all learned our lessons well, and victims not infrequently become fervent
abettors of their executioners, living in communion with the latter in a
closed, self-accredited universe of lies. But once more, *they* spoke. *They*
decide who is "racism-free or anti-colonial," and they seriously think they
can go on formulating criteria for us, telling us where and how to detect
what they seem to know better than us: racism and colonialism. Natives
must be taught in order to be anti-colonialist and de-westernized; they are,
indeed, in this world of inequity, the handicapped who cannot represent
themselves and have to either be represented or learn how to represent
themselves. Whatever the issue, they are entrapped in a circular dance
where they always find themselves a pace behind the white saviors. I am
tired of being blamed for my ancestors' mistakes. Stop wallowing in the
past. Haven't you heard these lines before? Language has myriad key-
sentences that generously inspire you despite yourself. Then, why continue to aspire after the colonial order of their language? The past? Past
to whom? They strip your identity off and paste it back on, calling it
your creative aspect of "revitalization," a positive affirmation of your
own cultural traditions, heritage, and identity, which will also, obviously
(how can they miss that?), be of potential significance for anthropological
analysis of culture change. Gone out of date, then revitalized, the mission
of civilizing the savage mutates into the imperative of "making equal."
This is how aliens form aliens, how men in crisis succeed to study
men in crisis.

A Myth of mythology

Treating the indigene as object achieves only the first of the three steps
instituted by the Great Master as essential to every scientific anthropological investigation. Once the skin is acquired, the flesh and bone
can only be reached through participation in the life and thought of the
native. "Social facts do not reduce themselves to scattered fragments. They
are lived by men, and subjective consciousness is as much a form of their
reality as their objective characteristics."[19] These are the lines flowing from
the pen of a well-known modern anthropologist, one of the few who have
intermittently acknowledged, first, that writing cannot cross (out or over)

writing without questioning the material (here, language) that defines it and, second, that anthropology which expresses itself in discourse cannot remain unaware (or willingly ignorant) of the "nature" of discourse. He is also one of the few who have opened up a self/other-referential language space where the observing-writing subject watches himself observe and write (this has little in common with the so-called self-knowledge and self-criticism aiming at "improvement"). He has admitted openly that his analysis of two hundred South American myths (by translating these myths into intellectual terms, has caused a transmutation and) should be read as a "myth of mythology."[20] Letting his pen run along the cleft of the perfect double that unveils *perfect* as illusion, this modern anthropologist reasons that "however scrupulous and objective he [the ethnographer] may want to be, it is never either himself or the other whom he encounters at the end of his investigation." What he experiences is, rather, what he calls "the superposition of himself on the other."[21] This insistent finger on the open wound has infuriated more than one among his colleagues. White academicians accuse white academicians of being academic and ethnocentric. The same accusations bounce back and forth under the banner of humanity and equality for the natives. The civilized man has become a problem to the civilized man, and he who shows himself naked with his speech or says out loud that the emperor has no clothes should expect his peers to call him an exhibitionist. Speaking about the average member of any society in the past and especially the "present-day savage," the Great Master asserted: "The lower his level of cultural development, the greater stickler he will be for good manners, propriety and form, and the more incomprehensive and odious to him will be the non-conforming point of view." If "the main social force governing all tribal life could be described as the inertia of custom,"[22] then tribalism is undoubtedly in full bloom among present-day academicians. Numerous scholars in the field have not missed the opportunity to manifest their hostility toward this modern anthropologist and blame him for looming larger than the people observed in his writings. No more illusory reflection; rather, *superposition* of *two presences,* hence the perpetual fear of one presence absorbing the other. What emerges again is the fear mentioned earlier—a one-way assimilation that resolves into a one-way assimilation of the Other. Here, you still exist and I do too, but one of us is bound to remain the shadow of the other, otherwise I run the risk of "going over the hill." Thus:

> Leaving his country and his home for long periods; exposing himself to hunger, sickness and occasional danger; allowing his habits, his beliefs, his conviction to be tampered with, conniving at this, indeed, when, without mental reservations or ulterior motives [sic], he assumes the modes of life of

a strange society, the anthropologist practises total observation, beyond which there is nothing except—and there *is* a risk—the complete absorption of the observer by the object of his observation.[23]

From the exact, unmisted reflection to the superposition of oneself on the other, the problem remains the same. The vanity of Metaphysics has the merit of marking time: it leads one straight back to the positivist dream of pure truth and pure presence. Naked, but not naked enough, I would say. The language of Buddhism sometimes speaks of the eighty-four thousand entrances to reality, and thinking reality versus non-reality may also lead to one of them as long as this chatter of the soul doesn't take the finger pointing at the moon for the moon itself.

He who represents his own discourse on myths as a myth is acutely aware of the illusion of all reference to a subject as absolute center. The packaging of myths must somehow bear the form of that which it attempts to enclose, if it wishes to come closest to its object. One cannot seize without smothering, for the will to freeze (capture) brings about a frozen (emptied) object. The modern anthropologist no longer believes in the naïve subjection of language—a locus of traditions and thinking habits whose historical dimensions he/we can never master. His understanding of myths through language leads, therefore, to a mythological "mythomorphic" discourse, which reveals myths functioning like syntagms within a system in perpetual motion, "communicating with each other *by means of men without men knowing it.*"

> There is no real end to methodological analysis [of myths], no hidden unity to be grasped once the breaking down process has been completed. Themes can be split up *ad infinitum.* Just when you think you have disentangled and separated them, you realize that they are knitting together again in response to the operation of unexpected affinities. Consequently the unity of the myth is never more than tendential and projective. . . . It is a phenomenon of the imagination, resulting from the attempt at interpretation.[24]

Anonymous myths give birth to other anonymous myths, multiplying and ramifying themselves without the fear of one being absorbed by the other, and beyond any myth teller's control. Like leaves of grass, they grow and die following the rhythm of impermanent-permanent nature. I who deceptively donate myself to any single master setting about to conquer me have no real master. For, the underdeveloped is first and foremost someone who believes in development. Myths circulate like gifts without givers, and no myth teller (cares to) knows where they come from or who invented them; "whatever their real origins, they exist only as elements embodied in tradition." The same myth varies widely from one teller to another and "yet the natives do not seem to worry about this state of affairs."[25] Why would they, indeed? Who sets off searching for "real origins"? Who suffers from the need for classification and identification? Who strives for identity, a certain identity? Questions are always loaded with the questioner's prejudices. Since there is "no hidden unity to be grasped," no secret meaning to discover behind the package, to look for it is to throw the package away. A thoughtful white man apparently came closest to native myth telling when he wrote: "The most 'realistic' work will not be the one which 'paints' reality, but one which, using the world as content, will explore as profoundly as possible the *unreal reality* of language."[26] More "realistic" than many of his colleagues, the modern anthropologist thus explains his undertaking:

> I therefore claim to show, not how men think in myths, but how myths operate in men's minds *without their being aware of the fact.* . . . what I am concerned to clarify is not so much what there is *in* myths (without, incidentally, being in man's consciousness) as the system of axioms. . . . As the myths themselves are based on secondary codes (the primary codes being those that provide a substance of language), the present work is put forward as a tentative draft of a tertiary code, which is intended to ensure the reciprocal translatability of several myths.[27] (my italics)

The tertiary code is at the same time unconscious and rational. Achieved through a systematic breaking-down process, a weaving of unexpected affinities, and an attempt at interpretation, deciphering the tertiary code is a direct result of "total observation." The practice of such observation, according to the modern anthropologist, consists in alternating between two methods, the empirical and deductive, and carrying each to its extreme.[28] One may deduce that the anthropologist's task is to superpose in him both the *bricoleur* (the man who works with any tools at hand) and the engineer (the man who works with tools he creates anew). The latter is said "to question the universe, while the *bricoleur* addresses himself to a collection of oddments left over from human endeavours, that is, only a sub-set of the culture."[29] The constant oscillation between these two distinct, absorption-resistant presences should eventually give birth to an anthropo-logical discourse that sometimes does not pretend to anything other than "a kind of intellectual 'bricolage' "—whose rules are "to make do with . . . a set of tools and materials which is always finite and is also heterogeneous because what it contains bears no relation to the current project"[30]—and other times claims to be exactly the opposite, that is to say, constructed anew in its totality—which, in language, involves syntax and lexicon. *Bricolage* is to engineering what common sense is to (the Great Master's definition of) the scientific mind. A discourse that legitimizes itself as scientific unavoidably bears within it a critique of *bricolage;* yet whatever the "brilliant unforeseen results" arrived at, there is not one single anthropological study that does not proceed from and does not take on the form of an intellectual *bricolage* whose information may always be re-ordered, completed, or refuted by further research. The image conveyed through this discourse of "total observation" is, therefore, either that of a *bricolage* aspiring vainly after the engineer's scientism or that of an engineering constantly annulling itself through *bricolage* without being able to dispense with it. The problem implied in this unresolvable contradiction has been raised by a philosopher more precisely as follows:

> A subject who supposedly would be the absolute origin of his own discourse and supposedly would construct it "out of nothing," "out of whole cloth," would be the creator of the verb, the verb itself. The notion of the engineer who supposedly breaks with all forms of *bricolage* is therefore a theological idea . . . the odds are that the engineer is a myth produced by the *bricoleur.* As soon as we cease to believe in such an engineer and in a discourse which breaks with received historical discourse, and as soon as we admit that every finite discourse is bound by a certain *bricolage* and that the engineer and the scientist are also species of *bricoleurs,* then the very idea of *bricolage* is menaced and the difference in which it took on its meaning breaks down.[31]

Bouncing back and forth from one opposite to another, *total* thus reveals its essence to be mainly *bricolage.* It is a *bricolage* that courts lingering dissatisfaction, since the question raised, "How (much more) total can (my) observation be?" will remain unanswerable. Surely the modern anthropologist has shed invaluable light on the farthest cellar corners of the anthropo-logical mind and its numerous dusty, willingly-kept-in-oblivion shelves. But he does so with an acute feeling of loss that trickles through the pages of his thought. In his longing for an impossible totalization which he sometimes claims and sometimes rejects as a "grave mistake,"[32] he separates the man "who works by means of signs"—the *bricoleur*—from the man "who works by means of concepts"—the engineer—to better appropriate the two to himself. Divide and conquer. The anthropologist as humanist-scientist is therefore the (still) longed-for offspring of a marriage of convenience between the physical and the human sciences:

> whereas concepts aim to be wholly transparent with respect to reality, signs allow and even require the interposing and incorporation of a certain amount of human culture into reality. . . . Both approaches are equally valid. Physics and chemistry are already striving to become qualitative again. . . .

Mythical thought . . . also acts as a liberator by its protest against the idea that anything can be meaningless with which science at first resigned itself to a compromise.[33]

The positivist yearning for transparency with respect to reality is always lurking below the surface. The world of concepts separates itself from the world of signs, as if thinker could be conceived apart from thought and beyond it; as if science which comes about through the element of discourse could simply cross over discourse and create a world of its own without giving up the series of rational and empirical operations that make it up. No concepts function without signs—sign being both thinker and thought. No engineer can ever render the finger pointing to the moon so transparent as to turn it into the moon itself. As soon as we recognize the unreality of such a separation, the difference that allows concept and sign to take on their meanings crumbles and the dream of transparency returns to the void. So does the scientist who establishes this convenient division and marriage, but does not hesitate to voice elsewhere[34] his inclination to define man, not as a *Homo faber*, a tool maker, but an inheritor of language, that is to say, a system of signs. How can one ever come close to a general concept of the Human Being, we may then ask, when one still believes in escaping (even temporarily) the human while studying the human? In formalizing without anthropologizing?

What "man" and which "man"?

Anthropology emerging as a semiology, the "study of the life of signs at the heart of social life," may recover lost common sense by ridding itself of its pretensions to simply be what the modern anthropologist calls "a conversation of man with man."[35] Simplicity, however, has its own exactingness, and the questions immediately raised here will be: What "man" and which "man"? It seems clear that the favorite object of anthropological study is not just *any* man but a specific kind of man: the Primitive, now elevated to the rank of the full yet needy man, the Native. Today, anthropology is said to be "conducted in two ways: in the pure state and in the diluted state." He who devotes himself to "pure" anthropology should not "confuse its object with other objects," for this "is not the source of action resulting from a sound scientific attitude." He should make a clear distinction between his profession and that of the sociologist by concentrating on those native societies whose distance and "differences in nature . . . [with] our own" privilege observation, making of field research "the mother and wet nurse of doubt, the philosophical attitude par excellence." It is by this "strictly philosophical method," this "anthropological doubt," which consists of "exposing what one thought one knew . . . to the buffetings and denials which are directed at one's most cherished ideas and habits by other ideas and habits,"[36] that anthropology distinguishes itself from sociology. Such a definition of "pure" anthropology and its requisite living laboratories offers a satisfactory answer to the question "what man?" Two seemingly clashing sets of signs take on their meanings through a difference that emerges from the same site; two cultures become culture through the same eye. The search for a purer original state (an influential anthropologist paradoxically wrote: "The romance of native cultures, to the anthropologist, lies [not in their unspoiled noble-savage-aspect but] in what they disclose about the *roots* of human behavior" [my italics]),[37] and the emphasis laid on a self-challenging, self-present state of alertness speak for the internal consistency of anthropology. Here, the gap between the modern anthropologist and the Great Master seems to close, since the study of the native's mind and behavior is, as quoted from the Great Master earlier, only worth pursuing when it is carried out with the hope that "we shall have some light shed on our own" and that "man's mentality will be revealed to us." Variations on this theme will appeal to you as follows: I am attracted to the Other because of (certain specific) affinities that exist between me and this Other, or "the essential vocation of interpretive anthropology is not to answer our deepest questions, but to make available to us answers that others, guarding other sheep in other valleys, have given, and thus to include them in the consultable record of what man has said."[38] The question remains whether this inclusion is disinterested or not. If it is not, as in this case— what is apparently aimed at is "to make available to us" who need it a "consultable record of what man has said"—the result will simply be the opposite or a by-product of "exclusion," and a stirring about within the same pattern of logic. The "conversation of man with man" is, therefore, mainly a conversation of "us" with "us" about "them," of the white man with the white man about the primitive-native man. The specificity of these three "man" grammatically leads to "men"; a logic reinforced by the modern anthropologist who, while aiming at the generic "man" like all his colleagues, implies elsewhere that in this context, man's mentality should be read as men's mentalities. Anthropologists, he declares, enjoy an advantage over their fellow men because they have grown into the habit of forgoing the comparing of two different systems of reference. They would not deserve the same tag they wear if they had not forbidden themselves to found their reasoning about their own society on observations coming from other societies.[39] The study of man is a study of men. It is, indeed, not uncommon to encounter in anthropological writings—in any man's writing, or perhaps I should say any human's writing—passages such as "the synthesis [of elements that constitute the native man's social existence], however approximate, arises from *human* experience. We must be sure of this, since *we study men*; and as *we are ourselves men*, we have that possibility" (my italics).[40] Since man can never be man but only men, since the uses of man and men are interchangeable, why not eliminate man for more consistency? Why hold on to its ambiguity and grammatical incorrectness?

If "man" is grammatically incorrect when used to designate two specific, irreducible "man"-signs, it is, however, grammatically perfectly correct when applied to include two non-specific, one-way reducible man-woman signs. This is where the question "which man?" arises. Which man, indeed? The one that "embraces woman" or the one that excludes her? The one defined as a human being or the one intended as a male human being? The further one proceeds, the less pertinent the question turns out to be, and the stronger the feeling of going round in a generic trap-circle. After all, the two "man" only appear inconsistent. They have, in fact, always supported and acted in collusion with each other. What can such a word as "human" mean when its collaboration with "man" and "men" throughout the history of *man*kind has become obvious? What can "human experience" imply in a "Men Only" context where *we who are ourselves men study men?* Listen, for example, to a doctor-man say how for years he had been fascinated by "the law in which man's ideas express what is essentially human in his nature."[41] "His," as some may continue to argue in all dishonesty, is here supposed to cover "her" too. And *"he,"* as an unqualified generic pronoun, can be used correctly to include "she," for *"He or she* does as much to combat sexism as a sign saying 'Negroes admitted' would do to combat racism."[42] Carried just a step further, such reasoning should logically lead to the assertion that whenever the word "white" is used, it means both white and black or white, black, yellow, and red. At least, hegemony will then throw off its mask, and language, the language of dominance, will reveal its paucity, flattening out all individualities, excluding all differences and blending, by the same token, the duping with the duped. Women, like colored, is the "lesser man," and as a Chinese-American woman remarks, "in America, Everyman—the universal human being—is white."[43] Obviously, no revolutionist says "white" intending it to include "colored." "White" has always been used to mean "white only or "non-Colored," although we all know that literally as well as figuratively, it can never pretend to eliminate colors without eliminating itself. The will to annihilate the Other through a false incorporation can be detected in every language sign that tends, by its ever-widening scope of encompassment, to be taken for granted. Such is the case of "nature," which normally goes hand in hand with "human" and "man," their lifelong friendship or dependency growing within the frame of the male-is-the-norm tradition of thought and, apparently, *without the men knowing it.* Imagine a world of *yang* and *yang* instead of *yin* (the female principle) and *yang* (the male principle)—a concept which in China never offers two absolute oppositions—and you will have the inhuman (hu)man-constructed world of Frankenstein. Nature, in such a container, will undoubtedly remain "his nature," a culturalized man-made product, which one may refer to as Father Nature. The supposedly universal tension between Nature and Culture is, in reality, a non-universal hu*man* dis-ease. No conflict exists between what has conventially been called Father Culture and Mother Nature, except when the pair are thought of as opposite to each other (instead of different from each other) so that Mother becomes a male-fashioned Mother exiled from culture, which is tantamount to saying Father Culture versus Father Nature. The logic functioning at the heart of this closed universe is a logic that fails to grasp the void in its creative potential and cannot view nothingness otherwise than as the permanent end of all/its existence. Thus, being and non-being have come to fear each other and act in mutual exclusiveness instead of mutual generation and support.

[is travel lit a form of anthropology]

Gossip and science: a conversation on what I love according to truth

A conversation of "us" with "us" about "them" is a conversation in which "them" is silenced. "Them" always stands on the other side of the hill, naked and speechless, barely present in its absence. Subject of discussion, "them" is only admitted among "us," the discussing subjects, when accompanied or introduced by an "us," member, hence the dependency of "them" and its need to acquire good manners for the membership standing. The privilege to sit at table with "us," however, proves both uplifting and demeaning. It impels "them" to partake in the reduction of itself and the appropriation of its otherness by a detached "us" discourse. The presence of a (grateful) witness serves to legalize such discourse, allowing it to mimic, whenever necessary, the voice of truth. Thus, "it is as if I saw my other dead, reduced, shelved in an urn upon the wall of the great mausoleum of language."[44] All admittance of "them" among "us" is a hoax; a false incorporation that leaves "them" barer than ever, if "them" allows itself to nibble at the bait of Lies. The anthropologist-nativist who speaks "about them" and "for them" is like the man who "strikes a mouse with a stick he doesn't want to soil!" (Chinese proverb). The conversation he aspires to turns out to be rather intimate: a chatty talk, which, under cover of cross-cultural communication, simply superposes one system of signs over another. Anthropology is finally better defined as "gossip" (we speak together about others) than as "conversation" (we discuss a question), a definition that dates back to Aristotle.[45] This profuse, idle talk between kinsmen (from the Old English *godsibb*) comes into being through boredom and the need to chat. An African man has perhaps best depicted the amorous link binding these men when he writes: "[Anthropology] has become a homily, a pretentious discourse that illustrates the fundamental misery of the industrialized man. . . . Colonialization [Nativism] is scientific because the colonized [the native] is scientifically comprehended."[46] The love-matching (hate-matching) of science and gossip is as ludicrous as the wedding of *bricolage* and engineering turns out to be. Scientific gossip takes place under relatively intimate conditions and mostly without witnesses; hence the gossipers' need to act in solidarity, leaning on and referring to each other for more credibility. The confidence they (re)gain through the ritual of citing all their fellows' (dead or living) names has allowed them to speak with the apathetic tone of the voice of knowledge. This is how gossip manages to mingle with science and, reciprocally, "when knowledge, when science speaks, I sometimes come to the point of hearing its discourse as the sound of a gossip which describes and disparages lightly, coldly, and objectively what I love: which speaks of what I love *according to truth.*"[47] Gossip's pretensions to truth remain however very peculiar. The kind of truth it claims to disclose is a confidential truth that requires commitment from both the speaker and the listener. He who lends an ear to gossip already accepts either sympathizing with or being an accomplice of the gossiper. Scientific gossip, therefore, often unveils itself as none other than a form of institutionalized Indiscretion. To grasp the tightly knit strength of Nativist discourse is to perceive the mechanisms it develops in its defense and validation of a certain ethic of obtrusiveness.

The anthropologist-nativist who seeks to perforate meaning by forcing his entry into the Other's personal realm undertakes the desperate task of filling in all the fissures that would reveal the emptiness of knowledge. On the lookout for "messages" that might be wrested from the object of study, in spite of its opacity or its reticence in sharing its intimacy with a stranger, this knowledgeable man spends his time spying on the natives, in fear of missing any of these precious moments where the latter would be caught unaware, therefore still living. The more indiscreet the research, the greater the value of its revelation. Listen once again to the Great Master as he sets out to describe *The Sexual Life of Savages*.[48] Under the general heading of science and knowledge of man, there emerged a form of legal voyeurism appraised by the gossipers as a great advance toward a personal identification with the natives observed. Here, the Great Master proceeds to give his fellow men "an increasingly detailed view of native love-making," carefully exposing the difficulties of his fieldwork. In the treatment of such a "delicate subject, the ethnographer is bound to a large extent to depend on hearsay" and on information collected from "all the gossip of those not directly affected by the event, yet sufficiently interested in it to talk." Thus, village gossip figures among the "valuable material" that provides the investigator with the possibility of getting "a true perspective, and look-[ing] at matters from the native point of view." Handling "love in fiction or anthropology" is no easy task for a voyeur who aspires to scientism. The solution offered is, therefore, a regular insertion of light, cold, objective remarks between novelistic descriptions, which coherently reconstruct, from A to Z and even with some feelings and passion, the love-making scene. What is put forth is not the interpretive aspect—the gathering of details through gossip—but the observational aspect, which does not fail to give the reader the feeling of being the accomplice of a voyeur hidden behind some wall or bush, taking delight in seeing and appropriating two lovers' utmost intimate acts. Many other rhetorical manipulations may be further detected. One of the erotic approaches the Great Master discussed so as "to satisfy a general curiosity on this point" is, for example, the kiss:

> Students of anthropology, as well as frequenters of comic opera, know that *even* in such high civilizations as those of China and Japan the kiss as a gesture in the art of love is unknown. A European shudders at the idea of such cultural deficiency. For his comfort, it may be said at once that things are not so black as they look. (my italics)

After having thus selected his public and explained why he undertook such a project, the Great Master set about making a distinction between the European and the Trobriand kiss, referring to the latter in terms of "lip activities." The same remark applies to his description of the lover's passionate or tender biting off of his mistress's eyelashes, which concludes flatly (scientifically, in his opinion) as follows: "It shows that the eye to them is an object of active bodily interest." Such rhetorical reductions betray a belief that confuses the knowledge of an act with the act itself; it is what an interpretive(ist) anthropologist calls "the cognitive fallacy," which tends "to identify winking with eyelid contractions or sheep raiding with chasing woolly animals out of pastures."[49] In his yearning for scientific truth and objectivity, the Great Master recurrently defended the

validity of his analysis by insisting on his will to confirm all *ad hoc* information "from a number of concrete instances." His impressions, as he asserted, "were constantly checked . . . by data drawn from every sphere
of tribal life. In fact, chronologically, the 'documents' are usually obtained first, but their real comprehension can be gained only from the knowledge of real life." The ambiguity of such declarations leaves the reader
once more uncertain as to both the true nature (which he always claim-
ed to see in objects he studied) of his "concrete instances," "every
sphere of tribal life," "real comprehension," and the ability, in his own
words, "to see things as they are, in opposition to what our fancy
would like them to be," if this "knowledge of real life" is gained without his witnessing the intimate facts himself. At no moment during this
long verbal demonstration on the savages' sexual life did the Great
Master seem to realize that he, like the (unaware) informants who "gossip about other people's business, and especially about their love affairs," was likewise gossiping and that his reconstruction of other people's reconstructions of their peers' intrigues might be best designated
as gossip about gossip.

Nativist interpretation

Anthropological writings have been equated with fiction. Yet, when the
Great Master places the two words—anthropology and fiction—next to
each other (as quoted earlier) in his analysis, one may deduce that, in view
of his scientific yearnings, he either made a mistake, failed to notice this
slip of the pen (not being aware of the possible connotations of such a
juxtaposition), or unconsciously let out an avowal. The writings can indeed
be defined as fiction from the standpoint of a certain concept of subjectivity. An analysis of the other-not-me (or of oneself) does not occur without
the intervention of the me (or of one's "higher" self), and the division
between the observer and the observed. The search for meaning will
always arrive at a meaning through I. I, therefore, am bound to acknowledge the irreducibility of the object studied and the impossibility of deliver-
ing its presence, reproducing it *as it is* in its truth, reality, and otherness.
The dilemma lies in the fact that descriptions of native life, although not
necessarily false or unfactual, are "actor-oriented," that is to say, recon-
structed or fashioned according to an individual's imagination. It also,
however, lies in the fact that descriptions are actor-oriented by their very
nature. Anthropological writings can therefore further be determined as
fictions from the standpoint of language. They assume, through a system
of signs, a possibility as a fact, irrespective of its actuality as sign. Science
fiction always comforts in its inventions, for it never circulates outside

men's image-repertoire. Outer-space creatures not only result from a compromise between humans and animals, they, very naturally, also speak
men's languages. Here is where the limit of human imagination most
conspicuously delineates itself: all the modern technologies displayed cannot suffice to overcome its creative "deficiency" as long as these somehow
inhuman or above-human creatures continue to use our human system
of signs exactly the way we use it, loading it with the same values
and prejudices. Descriptions or clinical inventories, whatever the chosen
mode of utterance, are fictional because language itself is fictional. In reflection, "fiction" may after all be used interchangeably with "jargon,"
for:

> Every fiction is supported by a social jargon, a sociolect, with which it
> identifies: fiction is that degree of consistency a language attains when it has
> jelled exceptionally and finds a sacerdotal class (priests, intellectuals, artists)
> to speak it generally and to circulate it.

In its rivalry with other fictions,

> each jargon (each fiction) fights for hegemony; if power is on its side, it
> spreads everywhere in the general and daily occurrences of social life, it
> becomes *doxa*, nature: this is the supposedly apolitical jargon of politicians,
> of agents of the State, of the media, of conversation.[50]

To say that man is above all *Homo significans*, that culture is essentially a
semiotic concept, webs of significance man has himself spun, and that
anthropological writings are interpretations and *only* interpretations is not
enough. One should remain consistent with one's scientific endeavor and
further inquire into the "nature" of these interpretations. For although no
writing can escape interpretation and ethnocentrism, obviously not all
openly interpretive anti-ethnocentric writings are of equal pertinence. Anthropology as a semiology should itself be treated in semiological terms. It
should situate its position and function in the system of meaning or, in
other words, explicitly assume a critical responsibility towards its own
discourse, exposing its status as inheritor of the very system of signs it sets
out to question, disturb, and shatter. Very few anthropological writings,
however, maintain a critical language and even fewer carry within themselves a critique of (their) language. A subversion of the colonizer's ability
to represent colonized cultures (albeit in interpretation rather than in direct
observation) can only radically challenge the established power relations
when it carries with it a tightly critical relation with the colonizer's most
confident characteristic discourses. To say that reality is always adaptive is
not necessarily to deny the referential function of language but to explicitly
acknowledge that the proper referent of any account is no more the

represented world than the specific instances of (anthropological) discourse. Interpretive anthropology does not offer any important change of venue as long as negative knowledge about the constituted authority of linguistic utterance is not made available in the very process of meaning and interpreting. Such a critical practice necessitates a questioning and shifting (in anthropology) of the very notion of "science" as objective understanding or study of systematized knowledge.

How do anthropological interpretations differ from any other interpretation? An interpretive anthropologist determines that "they are anthropological—that is part of a developing system of scientific analysis . . . because it is, in fact, anthropologists who profess them."[51] The subjectivity involved here is not that of the individual but that of the anthropologist species. He who lays stress on the professional aspect of his work and defines himself essentially as a member of an institutionalized body of specialists capable of developing "a system of scientific analysis" spends his time searching exclusively for the stereotype in the Other. At no time, while he sets out scientifically to interpret the natives as bearers of a stamp imprinted on them "by the institutions in which they live, by the influence of tradition and folk-lore, by the very vehicle of thought, that is, by language,"[52] does he feel the scientific urge to specify where he himself stands, as a stereotype of his community, in his interpretation. Should he realize the impossibility of exhausting his subject—for, "cultural analysis is intrinsically incomplete. And, worse than that, the more deeply it goes the less complete it is"—he would simply reply that "interpretive anthropology is a science whose progress is marked less by a perfection of consensus than by a refinement of debate. What gets better is the precision with which we vex each other."[53] Haven't we seen earlier that anthropology is a matter of paying off old scores among a certain milieu of gossipers? A milieu that clings to science with the despair of a castaway. Being no more than a subject for anthropological gossip, the native, whose humanity figures in a "consultable record," simply serves to sow the seeds of scholarly suspicion, refining thereby the nativist debate while allowing the nativist lineage to live on. It is to be expected that the man who thus defines interpretive anthropology is the same to radically assert:

> We are not, or at least I am not, seeking either to become natives (a compromised word in any case) or to mimic them. Only romantics or spies would seem to find point in that. We are seeking, in the widened sense of the term in which it encompasses very much more than talk, to converse with them, a matter a great deal more difficult, and not only with strangers, than is commonly recognized. . . . the aim of anthropology is the enlargement of the universe of human discourse.[54]

If one turns a blind eye to the self-congratulating, patronizing (but refined) tone of this claim for a *conversation with them*, one may interpret such a declaration as a refutation of an ideal set up by the Great Master, which has remained since then profoundly anchored in the anthropological milieu. The ultimate goal of every ethnographer, the Great Master wrote, is "to grasp the native's point of view . . . to realise *his* vision of *his* world."[55] However elusive it proves to be, this line has become the famous formula of nativist belief, the anthropological creed par excellence. In other words, skin, flesh, and bone—or, if one prefers the Great Master's terms in a reverse order: skeleton, flesh-blood, and spirit—are not enough; the anthropologist should go beyond and reach for that "subjective desire . . . of realising the substance of their [the natives'] happiness," which, according to my own progression, may be considered "the *marrow* of native life." Can any discourse on man sound more homiletic than this scientific "conversation with them?" Keeping such cannibal-anthropological rites in mind, one can only assent to the following remark by an African man: "today . . . the only possible ethnology is the one which studies the anthropophagous behavior of the white man."[56]

See them as they see each other

To see the natives "as they see each other," the anthropologist should be able intermittently to "become the natives." Is this possible? How can one be a Nuer or a Trobriander? These are questions committed students in anthropology have unavoidably asked, even though many others chose and still choose to bypass them for fear of having to deal with a proliferation of complementary questions, which, in the process, are bound to shake anthropology down to its very foundation. Here, the Great Master answered he would not try "to cut or untie this knot, that is to say, to solve the problem *theoretically*" (my italics). First, he thought it was merely his "duty" as an anthropologist, to achieve such a goal, for "the natives obey the forces and commands of the tribal code, but they do not comprehend them; exactly as they obey their instincts and their impulses, but could not lay down a single law of psychology."[57] (Remember, anthropologists always set out to depict that which the natives live or carry on in their lives "without their knowing it" and to see through the latter's eyes with, in addition, God's grasp of the totality.) Second, he prescribed among various "*practical* means to overcome the difficulties involved," the acquisition of a knowledge of the native language. Language as a "system of social ideas" allows he who knows how it is used and uses it himself as "an instrument of inquiry" to render "the verbal contour of native thought as precisely as possible." The anthropologist's expertise in interpretation gains in scientific recognition as it now swells with the ambition of being also a loyal recording and translation of native mentality. In other words, language is a means through which an interpreter arrives at the rank of a scientist. The omniscient anthropologist "has to talk with [the native] under all sorts of conditions and to write down his words," for "after all, if natives could furnish us with correct, explicit and consistent accounts of their tribal organisation, customs and ideas, there would be no difficulty in ethnographic work."[58] The same rationale holds true when reversed, that is to say, when one acquires a knowledge of the anthropological-nativist language. If only he (the anthropologist) could provide us with correct, consistent accounts of himself, his gossiping organization, and the specific instances of discourse that constitute his very accounts, then there would be no need for us to carry out an ongoing critique of ethnographic ideology and its claim to represent other cultures. I say *us*, for there are and will be more and more voices to denounce this encratic language (a word borrowed from a thoughtful white man, "encratic" means the language produced and spread under the protection of power),[59] whose pressure lies not so much in its systematization and argumentation as in its unconscious "stickiness." In order to judge (by his own standards) how successful the Great Master was in his realization of the natives' vision of their world and his pretension, as "true interpreter of the Native," to "make clear to traders, missionaries and exploiters what the Natives really need and where they suffer most under the pressure of European interference,"[60] we can quote here two voices. The first comes from a Catholic missionary who spent thirty years in the Trobriands and is known to have mastered the language, the second from a Trobriander himself:

> I was surprised at the number of times informants helping me with checking [the Great Master] would bridle. . . . They did not quarrel with facts or explanation, only with the colouring, as it were. The sense expressed was not the sense they had of themselves, or of things Boyowan.

> I would point to the political nature of anthropology, in that it . . . carries a biased picture of those who read it. . . . if we are going to depend on anthropological studies to define our history and our culture and our "future," then we are *lost*.[61]

One need not, in fact, read the Great Master's *Diary* posthumously published to perceive the "reluctant imperialist" behind the falsely radical interpreter of the Native's need, but the diary confirms one's sense of the contempt for the "*niggers*" (his italics) that pierces through the professional writings despite his use there of the word "native," of fierce hatred for the "bloody negroes" whose life is "utterly devoid of interest or importance,

Trying to find the other by defining otherness or by explaining the other through laws and generalities is, as Zen says, like beating the moon with a pole or scratching an itching foot from the outside of a shoe (Stills from **I-C**)

something as remote to me as the life of a dog." Nor does one need to read the *Diary* to sense that beside their career-exploitable values, "ethnographical problems don't preoccupy me at all. At bottom I am living outside of Kiriwina, although strongly hating the *niggers*"; and to guess that the man who gossiped about others' modes of intercourse was a man isolated from the natives and deprived of intercourse, who used his ethnographic work to remedy his utter *boredom* with native life.[62] A patient reading of any of his writings suffices to reveal it riddled with prejudices as well as scientific-al-professional-scholarly-careerist hypocrisy. No anthropological under-taking can ever open up the other. Never the marrow. All he can do is wear himself out circling the object and define his other on the grounds of his being a man studying another man. How can he, indeed, read into the other knowing not how the other read into him? "Without a doubt," the modern anthropologist humbly admits, "the attempt will remain largely illusory: we shall never know if the other, into whom we cannot, after all, dissolve, fashions from the elements of his social existence a synthesis exactly superimposable on that which we have worked out."[63] The other is never to be known unless one arrives at a *suspension* of language, where the reign of codes yields to a state of constant non-knowledge, always un-derstanding that in Buddha's country (Buddha being, as some have de-fined, a clarity or an open space), one arrives without having taken a single step; unless one realizes what in Zen is called the Mind Seal or the continuous reality of awakening, which can neither be acquired nor lost; unless one understands the necessity of a practice of language which remains, through its signifying operations, a process constantly unsettling the identity of meaning and speaking/writing subject, a process never allowing I to fare without non-I. Trying to find the other by defining otherness or by explaining the other through laws and generalities is, as Zen says, like beating the moon with a pole or scratching an itching foot from the outside of a shoe. There is no such thing as a "coming face to face once and for all with objects"; the real remains foreclosed from the analytic experience, which is an experience of speech. In writing close to the other of the other, I can only choose to maintain a self-reflexively critical relation-ship toward the material, a relationship that defines both the subject written and the writing subject, undoing the I while asking "what do I want wanting to *know* you or me?"[64]

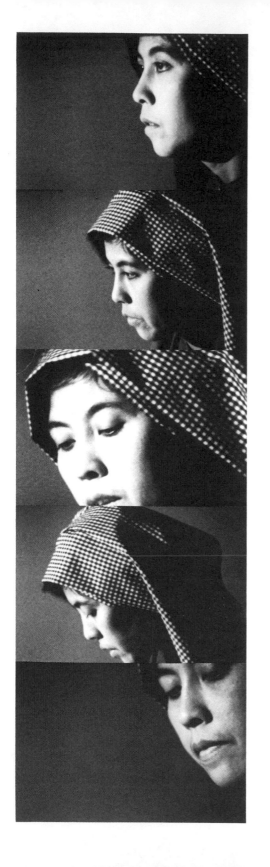

Women's liberation! You are still joking, aren't you? (Stills from **SVGNN***)*

III

Difference: "A Special Third World Women Issue"

It is thrilling to think—to know that for any act of mine, I shall get twice as much praise or twice as much blame. It is quite exciting to hold the center of the national stage, with the spectators not knowing whether to laugh or to weep

separate develme

—Zora Neale Hurston,
"How It Feels to Be Colored Me"

It must be odd
to be a minority
he was saying.
I looked around
and didn't see any.
So I said
Yeah
it must be.

—Mitsuye Yamada,
"Looking Out" in *Camp Notes*

Words empty out with age. Die and rise again, accordingly invested with new meanings, and always equipped with a secondhand memory. In trying to tell something, a woman is told, shredding herself into opaque words while her voice dissolves on the walls of silence. Writing: a commitment of language. The web of her gestures, like all modes of writing, denotes a historical solidarity (on the understanding that her story remains inseparable from history). She has been warned of the risk she incurs by letting words run off the rails, time and again tempted by the desire to gear herself to the accepted norms. But where has obedience led her? At best, to the satisfaction of a "made-woman," capable of achieving as high a mastery of discourse as that of the male establishment in power. Immediately gratified, she will, as years go by, sink into oblivion, a fate she inescapably shares with her foresisters. How many, already, have been condemned to premature deaths for having borrowed the master's tools and thereby played into his hands? Solitude is a common prerequisite, even though this may only mean solitude in the immediate surroundings. Elsewhere, in every corner of the world, there exist women who, despite the threat of rejection, resolutely work toward the unlearning of institutionalized language, while staying alert to every deflection of their body compass needles. *Survival*, as Audre Lorde comments, *"is not an academic skill. . . . It is learning how to take our differences and make them strengths. For the master's tools will never dismantle the master's house.* They may allow us temporarily to beat him at his own game, but they will never enable us to bring about genuine change."[1] The more one depends on the master's house for support, the less one hears what he doesn't want to hear. Difference is not difference to some ears, but awkwardness or incompleteness. Aphasia. Unable or unwilling? Many have come to tolerate this dissimilarity and have decided to suspend their judgments (only) whenever the other is concerned. Such an attitude is a step forward; at least the danger of speaking for the other has emerged into consciousness. But it is a very small step indeed, since it serves as an excuse for their complacent ignorance and their reluctance to involve themselves in the issue. You who understand the dehumanization of forced removal-relocation-reeducation-redefinition, the humiliation of having to falsify your own reality, your voice—you know. And often cannot *say* it. You try and keep on trying to unsay it, for if you don't, they will not fail to fill in the blanks on your behalf, and you will be said.

The policy of "separate development"

With a kind of perverted logic, they work toward your erasure while urging you to keep your way of life and ethnic values *within the borders of your homelands.* This is called the policy of "separate development" in apartheid language. Tactics have changed since the colonial times and indigenous cultures are no longer (overtly) destroyed (preserve the form but remove the content, or vice versa). You may keep your traditional law and tribal customs among yourselves, as long as you and your own kind are careful not to step beyond the assigned limits. Nothing has been left to chance when one considers the efforts made by the White South African authorities to distort and use the tools of Western liberalism for the defense of their racialistic-ally indefensible cause. Since no integration is possible when terror has become the order of the day, I (not you) will give you freedom. I will grant you autonomy—not complete autonomy, however, for "it is a liberal fallacy to suppose that those to whom freedom is given will use it only as foreseen by those who gave it."[2] (Confidentially, I live in a state of intense fear, knowing that Western education has taught you aggression in equality. Now I sleep with a gun under my pillow and lock

With time, it is between me and myself that silence settles down.
My intimacy is in silence. Still, I have to give advice to other
women who come looking for some light on their problems! (Stills
from **SVGNN**)

the gate at the top of my stairway; a single second of carelessness may cost me my life—for life and domination are synonyms to me—and I tremble at the slightest movement of my servants. Better intern you "for your own good" than be interned or "driven to the sea" by you.) Self-determination begins with the division of the land (on condition that I cut the cake), and I will make sure each of you gets the part s/he *deserves*. The delimitation of territories is my answer to what I perceive as some liberals' dream for "the inauguration, namely, of a system in which South Africa's many peoples would resolve themselves unreluctantly into one."[3] The governed do not (should not) compose a single people; this is why I am eager to show that South Africa is not one but ten separate nations (of which the White nation is the only one to be skin-defined; the other nine being determined largely on the basis of language—the Zulu nation, the Swazi nation, and so on). This philosophy—I will not call it "policy"—of "differentiation" will allow me to have better control over my nation while looking after yours, helping you thereby to gradually stand on your own. It will enable you to return to "where you belong" whenever you are not satisfied with my law and customs or whenever you are no longer useful to me. Too bad if you consider what has been given to you as the leftovers of my meals. Call it "reserves of cheap labor" or "bantustans" if you wish; "separate development" means that each one of us minds her/his own business (I will interfere when my rights are concerned since I represent the State) and that your economical poverty is of your own making. As for "the Asiatic cancer, which has already eaten so deeply into the vitals of South Africa, [it] ought to be resolutely eradicated."[4] Non-white foreigners have no part whatsoever in my plans and I "will undertake to drive the coolies [Indians] out of the country within four years."[5] My "passionate concern for the future of a European-type white society, and . . . that society's right to self-preservation" is not a question of color feeling, but of nationalism, the "Afrikaner nationalism [which] is a form of collective selfishness; but to say this is simply to say that it is an authentic case of nationalism."[6]

Words manipulated at will. As you can see, "difference" is essentially "division" in the understanding of many. It is no more than a tool of self-defense and conquest. You and I might as well not walk into this semantic trap which sets us up against each other as expected by a certain ideology of separatism. Have you read the grievances some of our sisters express on being among the few women chosen for a "Special Third World Women's Issue" or on being the only Third World woman at readings, workshops, and meetings? It is as if everywhere we go, we become Someone's private zoo. Gayatri Chakravorty Spivak spoke of their remarking "the maids upstairs in the guest quarters were women of color" in a symposium;[7] Gloria Anzaldúa, of their using her as a token woman and her friend Nellie Wong as a "purveyor of resource lists";[8] Mitsuye Yamada, of having to start from scratch each time, as if she were "speaking to a brand new audience of people who had never known an Asian Pacific woman who is other than the passive, sweet, etc., stereotype of the 'Oriental' woman";[9] Audre Lorde, of the lack of interracial cooperation between academic feminists whose sole explanation for the issue remains: "We did not know who to ask";[10] and Alice Walker, of the necessity of learning to discern the true feminist—"for whom racism is inherently an impossibility"—from the white female opportunist—"for whom racism, inasmuch as it assures white privilege, is an accepted way of life."[11] The decision you and I are called upon to make is fraught with far-reaching consequences. On the one hand, it is difficult for us to sit at table with them (the master and/or his substitutes) without feeling that our presence, like that of the "native" (who happens to be invited) among the anthropologists, serves to mask the refined sexist and/or racist tone of their discourse, reinforcing thereby its pretensions to universality. Given the permanent status of "foreign workers," we—like the South African blacks who are allowed to toil on white territories as "migrants," but are gotten rid of and resettled to the homeland area as soon as they become unprofitable labor units—continue in most cases to be treated as "temporary sojourners," even though we may spend our whole lifetime by their side pleading a common cause.

> the white rancher told Chato he was too old to work for him any more, and Chato and his old woman should be out of the shack by the next afternoon because the rancher had hired new people to work there. That had satisfied her. To see how the white man repaid Chato's years of loyalty and work. All of Chato's fine-sounding English didn't change things.[12]

The lines are an excerpt from Leslie Marmon Silko's "Lullaby." From the South African reserve to the American Laguna Pueblo Reservation, the story changes its backdrops but remains recognizable in the master's indifference to the lot of his non-European workers. Yet, on the other hand, you and I acquiesce in reviving the plot of the story, hoping thereby that our participation from the inside will empower us to act upon the very course of its events. Fools? It all depends on how sharply we hone ourselves on the edge of reality; and, I venture to say, we do it enough to never lose sight of our distinct actualities. Silence as a refusal to partake in the story does sometimes provide us with a means to gain a hearing. It is voice, a mode of uttering, and a response in its own right. Without other silences, however, my silence goes unheard, unnoticed; it is simply one voice less, or more point given to the silencers. Thus, no invitation is declined except in particular circumstances where we feel it is necessary to do so for our own well-being. What does it matter who the sponsor is? Every opportunity is fitted for consciousness raising; to reject it is almost tantamount to favoring apartheid ideology. White and black stand apart (armed legislation versus tribal law) and never the twain shall meet. There the matter rests. Crossed fears continue to breed wars, for they feed endlessly on each other until no conversation can possibly be carried out without heaping up misunderstandings. It is, indeed, much easier to dismiss or eliminate on the pretext of difference (destroy the other in our minds, in our world) than to live fearlessly with and within difference(s).

"What's the difference?" as if I cared? Or yes, I mean it, help me see? Shall I quench my thirst gazing at the plums while waiting for my helper to come by and pluck them off the branches for me? Do I really ask for difference or am I just saying it's not worth trying to find out? One of the classical questions our male world leaders used to throw out in interviews with feminists was: "If women are to be men's equals, how is it that history remains so short of female leaders' names?" (In other words, "Tell me, what is women's contribution to History?") Yes, and I also remember Virginia Woolf's bishop who convincingly declared in the papers that it was impossible for any woman, past, present, or to come, to have the genius of Shakespeare.[13] From the male reader-leader's standpoint, again, the great male writer-leader is matchless. Such a narrow-mindedness may sound quite outmoded today, for sexism no longer expresses itself as blatantly as it once did . . . and one somehow "feels sorry" for these men whose power extends well beyond the frontiers of their territories but whose field of vision ends at the fence of their own yard. Yet, it is this same ignorance and narrow-mindedness that lie behind answers similar to the one quoted above from academic feminists on the scarcity of Third World women's voices in debates: "We didn't know who to ask." Historians have, for several decades now, been repeating that History with a capital H does not exist and that it has never constituted the *a priori* reasoning of their discourse but, rather, its result. Like the anthropological study whose information may always be reordered, refuted, or completed by further research, the historical analysis is nothing other than the reconstruction and redistribution of a pretended order of things, the interpretation or even transformation of documents given and frozen into monuments. The re-writing of history is therefore an endless task, one to which feminist scholars have devoted much of their energy. The more they dig into the maze of yellowed documents and look into the non-registered facts of their communities, the more they rejoice upon discovering the buried treasures of women's unknown heritage. Such findings do not come as a godsend; they are gained through genuine curiosity, concern, and interest. Why not go and find out for yourself when you don't know? Why let yourself be trapped in the mold of permanent schooling and wait for the delivery of knowledge as a consumer waits for her/his suppliers' goods? The understanding of difference is a shared responsibility, which requires a minimum of willingness to reach out to the unknown. As Audre Lorde says,

> Women of today are still being called upon to stretch across the gap of male ignorance, and to educate men as to our existence and our needs. This is an old and primary tool of all oppressors to keep the oppressed occupied with the master's concerns. Now we hear that it is the task of black and third world women to educate white women, in the face of tremendous resistance, as to our existence, our differences, our relative roles in our joint survival. This is a diversion of energies and a tragic repetition of racist patriarchal thought.[14]

One has to be excessively preoccupied with the master's concerns, indeed, to try to explain why women cannot have written "the plays of Shakespeare in the age of Shakespeare," as Virginia Woolf did. Such a waste of energy is perhaps unavoidable at certain stages of the struggle; it need not, however, become an end point in itself.

"Why do we have to be concerned with the question of Third World women? After all, it is only one issue among many others." Delete "Third World" and the sentence immediately unveils its value-loaded clichés. Generally speaking, a similar result is obtained through the substitution of words like *racist* for *sexist*, or vice versa, and the established image of the *Third World Woman* in the context of (pseudo-) feminism readily merges with that of the *Native* in the context of (neo-colonialist) anthropology. The problems are interconnected. Here, a plural, angry reply may be expected: what else do you wish? It seems as if no matter what We do We are being resented. Now, "in response to complaints of exclusionary practices, special care is always taken to notify minority organizations and women of color of conferences, planning meetings, job openings, and workshops."[15] Once again, re-read the statement with the master's voice and with "woman" in place of "minority." Much remains to be said about the attitude adopted in this "special care" program and its (unavowed or unavowable) intent. Viewing the question through the eyes of a white sister, Ellen Pence thus writes:

> Gradually, I began to realize the tremendous gap between my rhetoric about solidarity with Third World women and my gut feelings. . . . Our idea of including women of color was to send out notices. We never came to the business table as equals. Women of color joined us on our terms. . . .
> I started seeing the similarities with how men have excluded the participation of women in their work through Roberts Rules of Order, encouraging us

to set up subcommittees to discuss *our* problems but never seeing sexism as their problem. It became clear that in many ways I act the same way toward women of color, supporting them in dealing with *their* issues. . . . I'm now beginning to realize that in many cases men do not understand because they have never committed themselves to understanding and by understanding, choosing to share their power. The lessons we've learned so well as women must be the basis for our understanding of ourselves as oppressive to the Third World women we work with.[16]

No matter which side i belong to, once i step down into the mud pit to fight my adversary, i can only climb out from it stained. This is the story of the duper who turns her/himself into a dupe while thinking s/he has made a dupe of the other. The close dependency that characterizes the master-servant relationship and binds the two to each other for life is an old, patent fact one can no longer deny. Thus, insofar as I/i understand how "sexism dehumanizes men," I/i shall also see how "my racism must dehumanize me" (Pence). The inability to relate the two issues and to feel them in my bones, has allowed me to indulge in the illusion that I will remain safe from all my *neighbors' problems* and can go on leading an undisturbed, secure life of my own. Hegemony and racism are, therefore, a pressing feminist issue; "as usual, the impetus comes from the grass-roots, activist women's movement." Feminism, as Barbara Smith defines it, "is the political theory and practice that struggles to free *all* women. . . . Anything less than this vision of total freedom is not feminism, but merely female self-aggrandizement."[17]

The sense of specialness

One gives "special care" to the old, to the disabled, and to all those who do not match the stereotype of the real wo/man. It is not unusual to encounter cases where the sense of specialness, which comes here with being the "first" or the "only" woman, is confused with the consciousness of difference. One cannot help feeling "special" when one figures among the rare few to emerge above the anonymous crowd and enjoys the privilege of preparing the way for one's more "unfortunate" sisters. Based on what other women are not (capable of) doing, such a reward easily creates a distance—if not a division—between I-who-have-made-it and You-who-cannot-make-it. Thus, despite my rhetoric of solidarity, I inwardly resist your entrance into the field, for it means competition, rivalry, and sooner or later, the end of my specialness. I shall, therefore, play a double game: on the one hand, I shall loudly assert my right, as a woman, and an exemplary one, to have access to equal opportunity; on the other

hand, I shall quietly maintain my privileges by helping the master perpetuate his cycle of oppression. The reasoning holds together only as long
as he does not betray me in my own game; and for that . . . I am bound to
breathe the same air he breathes, no matter how polluted it turns out to be.
My story, yours perhaps, that of Mitsuye Yamada, who describes herself
as:

> An Asian American woman thriving under the smug illusion that I was *not*
> the stereotypic image of the Asian woman because I had a career teaching
> English in a community college. I did not think anything assertive was
> necessary to make my point . . . it was so much my expected role that it
> ultimately rendered me invisible . . . contrary to what I thought, I had
> actually been contributing to my own stereotyping. . . . When the Asian
> American woman is lulled into believing that people perceive her as being
> different from other Asian women (the submissive, subservient, ready-to-
> please, easy-to-get-along-with Asian woman), she is kept comfortably con-
> tent with the state of things.[18]

and that of Adrienne Rich, who perceives her specialness as follows:

> My own luck was being born white and middle-class into a house full of
> books, with a father who encouraged me to read and write. So for about
> twenty years I wrote for a particular man, who criticized and praised me and
> made me feel I was indeed "special." The obverse side of this, of course, was
> that I tried for a long time to please him. . . .
> We seem to be special women here, we have liked to think of ourselves as
> special, and we have known that men would tolerate, even romanticize us as
> special, as long as our words and actions didn't threaten their privilege of
> tolerating or rejecting us and our work according to *their* ideas of what a
> special woman ought to be.[19]

There is more than one way to relate the story of specialness. I may
orient myself toward the same end by choosing a reasoning completely
opposite to the one mentioned above. Not only do I like to think of myself
as special but also as having a free hand. We all have the potential to be
special, I say, why not work for it? Let me *select* those with whom I would
like to share my blessings. Thus weaving my cocoon and closing myself
snugly, I then turn to my sisters and kindly urge them to proceed alike:
Weave your own cocoon; let it tie you in, in comfort, and I shall help to
gain that special, oh so special, recognition. Have you read Zora Neale
Hurston's "The 'Pet' Negro System?" The policy of "separate development" means that we may all bloom in our garden. It also means that i am
tolerated in my difference as long as i conform with the established rules.
Don't overstep the line. Considered both a "dangerous" species (remem-

ber the Yellow Peril in politicians' discourses and the descriptions of warlike savages in colonial reports. More subtly expressed today, the fear re-surfaces only when some Third World representatives become too outspoken), and an "endangered" species (suffering pathetically from a "loss of authenticity"), i am to remain behind the safety grille for the visitors' security and marvel. Specialness as a soporific soothes, anaesthetizes my sense of justice; it is, to the wo/man of ambition, as effective a drug of psychological self-intoxication as alcohol is to the exiles of society. Now, i am not only given the permission to open up and talk, i am also encouraged to express my difference. My audience expects and demands it; otherwise people would feel as if they have been cheated: We did not come to hear a Third World member speak about the First (?) World, We came to listen to that voice of difference likely to bring us *what we can't have* and to divert us from the monotony of sameness. They, like their anthropologists whose specialty is to detect all the layers of my falseness and truthfulness, are in a position to decide what/who is "authentic" and what/who is not. No uprooted person is invited to participate in this "special" wo/man's issue unless s/he "makes up" her/his mind and paints her/himself thick with authenticity. Eager not to disappoint, i try my best to offer my benefactors and benefactresses what they most anxiously yearn for: the possibility of a difference, yet a difference or an otherness that will not go so far as to question the foundation of their beings and makings. Their situation is not unlike that of the American tourists who, looking for a change of scenery and pace in a foreign land, such as, for example, Japan, strike out in search of what they believe to be the "real" Japan—most likely shaped after the vision of Japan as handed to them and reflected in television films like "Shogun"—or that of the anthropologists, whose conception of "pure" anthropology induces them to concentrate on the study of "primitive" ("native," "indigenous," or to use more neutral, technical terms: "non-state," "non-class") societies. Authenticity in such contexts turns out to be a product that one can buy, arrange to one's liking, and/or preserve. Today, the "unspoiled" parts of Japan, the far-flung locations in the archipelago, are those that tourism officials actively promote for the more venturesome visitors. Similarly, the Third World representative the modern sophisticated public ideally seeks is the *unspoiled* African, Asian, or Native American, who remains more preoccupied with her/his image of the *real* native—the *truly different*—than with the issues of hegemony, racism, feminism, and social change (which s/he lightly touches on in conformance to the reigning fashion of liberal discourse). A Japanese actually looks more Japanese in America than in Japan, but the "real" type of Japanism ought to be in Japan. The less accessible the product "made-in-Japan," the more trustworthy it is, and the greater the desire to acquire and protect it.

MIRROR MIRROR

People keep asking me where I come from
says my son.
Trouble is I'm american on the inside
          and   oriental on the outside
     No Doug
Turn that outside in
THIS is what America looks like.

—Mitsuye Yamada,
Camp Notes and Other Poems

The question of roots and authenticity

"I was made to feel," writes Joanne Harumi Sechi, "that cultural pride would justify and make good my difference in skin color while it was a constant reminder that I was different."[20] Every notion in vogue, including the retrieval of "roots" values, is necessarily exploited and recuperated. The invention of needs always goes hand in hand with the compulsion to help the needy, a noble and self-gratifying task that also renders the helper's service indispensable. The part of the savior has to be filled as long as the belief in the problem of "endangered species" lasts. To persuade you that your past and cultural heritage are doomed to eventual extinction and thereby keeping you occupied with the Savior's concern, inauthenticity is condemned as a *loss* of *origins* and a whitening (or faking) of non-Western values. Being easily offended in your elusive identity and reviving readily an old, racial charge, you immediately react when such guilt-instilling accusations are leveled at you and are thus led to stand in need of defending that very ethnic part of yourself that for years has made you and your ancestors the objects of execration. Today, planned authenticity is rife; as a product of hegemony and a remarkable counterpart of universal standardization, it constitutes an efficacious means of silencing the cry of racial oppression. We no longer wish to erase your difference, We demand, on the contrary, that you remember and assert it. At least, to a certain extent. Every path I/i take is edged with thorns. On the one hand, i play into the Savior's hands by concentrating on authenticity, for my attention is numbed by it and diverted from other, important issues; on the other hand, i do feel the necessity to return to my so-called roots, since they are the fount of my strength, the guiding arrow to which i constantly refer before heading for a new direction. The difficulties appear perhaps less insurmountable only as I/i succeed in making a distinction between difference reduced to identity-authenticity and difference understood also as critical difference from myself. The first induces an attitude of temporary tolerance—as exemplified in the policy of "separate development"—which serves to reassure the conscience of the liberal establishment and gives a touch of subversiveness to the discourse delivered. "That we may each have our due" or "that we may all have more" should, in *reality*, be read: "that I may not have any less." Hence, the (apartheid's) need to lay down (the) pass laws which restrict the "outsiders" freedom of movement as well as their choice of participation (only those whose discourse squares with that of the dominant are eligible), forcing them thereby to live in the reserves/ations. (Hence also, the widespread resistance against passes or "reference books" led by the black women, and their massive jailing in South Africa.) All "temporary sojourners," as observed in the more blatantly manifested case of South Africa, run the risk of being sent back to their homelands no matter how long they have been settled in the areas the Savior appropriates to her/himself. Differences that cause separation and suspicion therefore do not threaten, for they can always be dealt with as fragments. Mitsuye Yamada, a second-generation Asian American, relevantly remarks:

> our white sisters . . . should be able to see that political views held by women of color are often misconstrued as being personal rather than ideological. Views critical of the system held by a person in an "outgroup" are often seen as expressions of personal angers against the dominant society. (If they hate it so much here, why don't they go back?). . . .
> Many of us are now third and fourth generation Americans, but this makes no difference: periodic conflicts involving Third World peoples can abruptly change white Americans' attitudes towards us. . . . We found our status as true-blooded Americans was only an illusion in 1942 when we were singled out to be imprisoned for the duration of the war by our own government. . . . When I hear my students say, "We're not against the Iranians here who are mindful of their own business. We're just against those ungrateful ones who overstep our hospitality by demonstrating and badmouthing our government," I know they speak about me.[21]

Infinite layers: I am not i can be you and me

A critical difference from myself means that I am not i, am within and without i. I/i can be I or i, you and me both involved. We (with capital W) sometimes include(s), other times exclude(s) me. You and I are close, we intertwine; you may stand on the other side of the hill once in a while, but you may also be me, while remaining what you are and what i am not. The differences made *between* entities comprehended as absolute presences— hence the notions of *pure origin* and *true* self—are an outgrowth of a dualistic system of thought peculiar to the Occident (the "onto-theology" which characterizes Western metaphysics). They should be distinguished

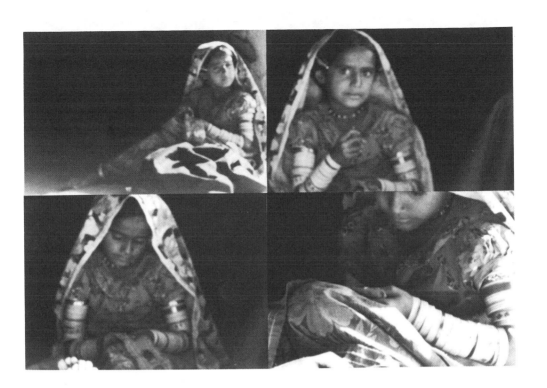

Between, within (Stills from **I-C**)

I/i can be I or i, you and me both involved. We sometimes includes, other times excludes me . . . you may stand on the other side of the hill once in a while, but you may also be me, while remaining what you are and what i am not (Stills from **R**)

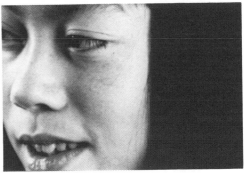

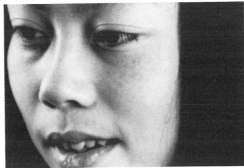

Difference undermines the very idea of identity (Stills from **SVGNN**)

from the differences grasped *both between* and *within* entities, each of these being understood as multiple presence.[22] Not One, not two either. "I" is, therefore, not a unified subject, a fixed identity, or that solid mass covered with layers of superficialities one has gradually to peel off before one can see its true face. "I" is, itself, *infinite layers*. Its complexity can hardly be conveyed through such typographic conventions as I, i, or I/i. Thus, I/i am compelled by the will to say/unsay, to resort to the entire gamut of personal pronouns to stay near this fleeing *and* static essence of Not-I. Whether I accept it or not, the natures of *I, i, you, s/he, We, we, they,* and *wo/man* constantly overlap. They all display a necessary ambivalence, for the line dividing *I* and *Not-I, us* and *them,* or *him* and *her* is not (cannot) always (be) as clear as we would like it to be. Despite our desperate, eternal attempt to separate, contain, and mend, categories always leak. Of all the layers that form the open (never finite) totality of "I," which is to be filtered out as superfluous, fake, corrupt, and which is to be called pure, true, real, genuine, original, authentic? Which, indeed, since all interchange, revolving in an endless process? (According to the context in which they operate, the superfluous can become the real; the authentic can prove fake; and so on.) *Authenticity* as a need to rely on an "undisputed origin," is prey to an obsessive *fear:* that of *losing a connection.* Everything must hold together. In my craving for a logic of being, I cannot help but loathe the threats of interruptions, disseminations, and suspensions. To begin, to develop to a climax, then, to end. To fill, to join, to unify. The order and the links create an illusion of continuity, which I highly prize for fear of nonsense and emptiness. Thus, a clear origin will give me a connection back through time, and I shall, by all means, search for that genuine layer of myself to which I can always cling. To abolish it in such a perspective is to remove the basis, the prop, the overture, or the finale—giving thereby free rein to indeterminancy: the result, forefeared, is either an anarchic succession of climaxes or a de(inex)pressive, uninterrupted monotony—and to enter into the limitless process of interactions and changes that nothing will stop, not even death. In other words, things may be said to be what they are, not exclusively in relation to what was and what will be (they should not solely be seen as clusters chained together by the temporal sequence of cause and effect), but also in relation to each other's immediate presences and to themselves as non/presences. The *real,* nothing else than a *code of representation,* does not (cannot) coincide with the lived or the performed. This is what Vine Deloria, Jr. accounts for when he exclaims: "Not even Indians can relate themselves to this type of creature who, to anthropologists, is the 'real' Indian."[23] A realistic identification with such a code has, therefore, no reality whatsoever: it is like "stopping the ear while trying to steal the bell" (Chinese saying).

WOMAN

It is a being somewhat like a well.
When you drop a well bucket
you will find
restlessness deep in the well. . . .

That she is herself
is more difficult than water is water
just as it's difficult for water to go beyond water
she and I are linked in mutual love
who once betrayed each other
two mirrors who reflected each other

When I escape from her, I incessantly
am forced to be her and when I confront her
instead I become him . . .

Korā Kumiko[24]

The female identity enclosure

Difference as uniqueness or special identity is both limiting and deceiving. If identity refers to the whole pattern of sameness within a human life, the style of a continuing me that permeates all the changes undergone, then difference remains within the boundary of that which distinguishes one identity from another. This means that *at heart,* X must be X, Y must be Y, and X *cannot* be Y. Those who run around yelling that X is not X and X *can* be Y usually land in a hospital, a "rehabilitation" center, a concentration camp, or a res-er-va-tion. All deviations from the dominant stream of thought, that is to say, the belief in a permanent essence of wo/man and in an invariant but fragile identity, whose "loss" is considered to be a "specifically human danger," can easily fit into the categories of the "mentally ill" or the "mentally underdeveloped." It is probably difficult for a "normal," probing mind to recognize that to seek is to lose, for seeking presupposes a separation between the seeker and the sought, the continuing me and the changes it undergoes. What if the popularized story of the identity crisis proves to be only a story and nothing else? Can identity, indeed, be viewed other than as a by-product of a "manhandling" of life, one that, in fact, refers no more to a consistent "pattern of sameness" than to an inconsequential process of otherness? How am I to lose, maintain, or gain an (fe/male) identity when it is impossible to me to take up a position outside this identity from which I presumably reach in and feel for it? Perhaps a way to portray it is to borrow these verses from the *Cheng-tao-ke:*

You cannot take hold of it,
But you cannot lose it.
In not being able to get it, you get it.
When you are silent, it speaks;
When you speak, it is silent.[25]

Difference in such an insituable context is *that which undermines the very idea of identity*, deferring to infinity the layers whose totality forms "I." It subverts the foundations of any affirmation or vindication of value and cannot, thereby, ever bear in itself an absolute value. The difference (within) between *difference* itself and *identity* has so often been ignored and the use of the two terms so readily confused, that claiming a female/ethnic identity/difference is commonly tantamount to reviving a kind of naïve "male-tinted" romanticism. If feminism is set forth as a demystifying force, then it will have to question thoroughly the belief in its own identity. To suppose, like Judith Kegan Gardiner, that "the concept of female identity provides a key to understanding the *special qualities* of contemporary writing by women . . ., the diverse ways in which writing by women *differs* from writing by men," and to "propose the preliminary metaphor 'female identity is a process' for the most fundamental of these differences" does not, obviously, allow us to radically depart from the master's logic. Such a formulation endeavors to "reach a theory of female identity . . . that *varies from the male model*," and to demonstrate that:

> primary identity for women is more flexible and relational *than for men.* Female gender identity is *more* stable *than male gender identity.* Female infantile identifications are *less* predictable *than male ones* . . . the *female counterpart* of the male identity crisis may occur more diffusely, at a different stage, or not at all. (my italics)

It seems quite content with reforms that, at best, contribute to the improvement and/or enlargement of the identity enclosure, but do not, in any way, attempt to remove its fence. The constant need to refer to the "male model" for comparisons unavoidably maintains the subject under tutelage. For the point is not to carve one's space in "identity theories that ignore women" and describe some of the faces of female identity, saying, like Gardiner: "I picture female identity as typically less fixed, less unitary, and more flexible than male individuality, both in its primary core and in the entire maturational complex developed from this core,"[26] but patiently to dismantle the very notion of core (be it static or not) and identity.

Woman can never be defined. Bat, dog, chick, mutton, tart. Queen, madam, lady of pleasure. MISTRESS. *Belle-de-nuit*, woman of the streets, fruitwoman, fallen woman. Cow, vixen, bitch. Call girl, joy girl, working girl. Lady and whore are both bred to please. The old Woman image-repertoire says She is a Womb, a mere baby's pouch, or "nothing but sexuality." She is a passive substance, a parasite, an enigma whose mystery proves to be a snare and a delusion. She wallows in night, disorder, and immanence and is at the same time the "disturbing factor (between men)" and the key to the beyond. The further the repertoire unfolds its images, the more entangled it gets in its attempts at capturing Her. "Truth, Beauty, Poetry—she is All: once more all under the form of the Other. All except herself,"[27] Simone De Beauvoir wrote. Yet, even with or because of Her capacity to embody All, Woman is the lesser man, and among male athletes, to be called a woman is still resented as the worst of insults. "Wo-" appended to "man" in sexist contexts is not unlike "Third World," "Third," "minority," or *color* affixed to *woman* in pseudo-feminist contexts. Yearning for universality, the generic "woman," like its counterpart, the generic "man," tends to efface difference within itself. Not every female is "a real woman," one knows this through hearsay . . . Just as "man" provides an example of how the part played by women has been ignored, undervalued, distorted, or omitted through the use of terminology presumed to be generic, "woman" more often than not reflects the subtle power of linguistic exclusion, for its set of referents rarely includes those relevant to Third World "female persons." "All the Women Are White, All the Blacks are Men, But Some of Us Are Brave" is the title given to an anthology edited by Gloria T. Hull, Patricia Bell Scott, and Barbara Smith. It is, indeed, somehow devious to think that WOMAN also encompasses the Chinese with bound feet, the genitally mutilated Africans, and the one thousand Indians who committed *suttee* for one royal male. Sister Cinderella's foot is also enviably tiny but never crooked! And, European witches were also burnt to purify the body of Christ, but they do not pretend to "self-immolation." "Third World," therefore, belongs to a category apart, a "special" one that is meant to be both complimentary and complementary, for First and Second went out of fashion, leaving a serious Lack behind to be filled.

Third World?

To survive, "Third World" must necessarily have negative *and* positive connotations: negative when viewed in a vertical ranking system—"underdeveloped" compared to over-industrialized, "underprivileged" within the already Second sex—and positive when understood sociopolitically as a subversive, "non-aligned" force. Whether "Third World" sounds negative or positive also depends on *who* uses it. Coming from you

Westerners, the word can hardly mean the same as when it comes from Us members of the Third World. Quite predictably, you/we who condemn it most are both we who buy in and they who deny any participation in the bourgeois mentality of the West. For it was in the context of such mentality that "Third World" stood out as a new semantic finding to designate what was known as "the savages" before the Independences. Today, hegemony is much more subtle, much more pernicious than the form of blatant racism once exercised by the colonial West. I/i always find myself asking, in this one-dimensional society, where I/i should draw the line between tracking down the oppressive mechanisms of the system and aiding their spread. "Third World" commonly refers to those states in Africa, Asia and Latin America which called themselves "non-aligned," that is to say, affiliated with neither the Western (capitalist) nor the Eastern (communist) power blocs. Thus, if "Third World" is often rejected for its judged-to-be-derogative connotations, it is not so much because of the hierarchical, first-second-third order implied, as some invariably repeat, but because of the growing threat "Third World" consistently presents to the Western bloc the last few decades. The emergence of repressed voices into the worldwide political arena has already prompted her (Julia Kristeva) to ask: "How will the West greet the awakening of the 'third world' as the Chinese call it? Can we [Westerners] participate, actively and lucidly, in this awakening when the center of the planet is in the process of moving toward the East?"[28] Exploited, looked down upon, and lumped together in a convenient term that denies their individualities, a group of "poor" (nations), having once sided with neither of the dominating forces, has slowly learned to turn this denial to the best account. "The Third World to Third World peoples" thus becomes an empowering tool, and one which politically includes all non-whites in their solidarist struggle against all forms of Western dominance. And since "Third World" now refers to more than the geographically and economically determined nations of the "South" (versus "North"), since the term comprises such "developed" countries as Japan and those which have opted for socialist reconstruction of their system (China, Cuba, Ethiopia, Angola, Mozambique) as well as those which have favored a capitalist mode of development (Nigeria, India, Brazil), there no longer exists such a thing as a unified unaligned Third World bloc. Moreover, Third World has moved West (or North, depending on where the dividing line falls) and has expanded so as to include even the remote parts of the First World. What is at stake is not only the hegemony of Western cultures, but also their identities as unified cultures. Third World dwells on diversity; so does First World. This is our strength and our misery. The West is painfully made to realize the existence of a Third World in the First World, and vice versa. The Master is bound to recognize that His Culture is not as homogeneous, as monolithic as He believed it to be. He discovers, with much reluctance, He is just an other among others.

Thus, whenever it is a question of "Third World women" or, more disquietingly, of "Third World Women in the U.S.," the reaction provoked among many whites almost never fails to be that of annoyance, irritation, or vexation. "Why Third World in the U.S.?" they say angrily; "You mean those who still have relatives in South East Asia?" "Third World! I don't understand how one can use such a term, it doesn't mean anything." Or even better, "Why use such a term to defeat yourself?" Alternatives like "Western" and "non-Western" or "Euro-American" and "non-Euro-American" may sound a bit less charged, but they are certainly neither neutral nor satisfactory, for they still take the dominant group as point of reference, and they reflect well the West's ideology of dominance (it is as if we were to use the term "non-Afro-Asian," for example, to designate all white peoples). More recently, we have been hearing of the Fourth World which, we are told, "is a world populated by indigenous people who still continue to bear a spiritual relationship to their traditional lands." The colonialist creed "Divide and Conquer" is here again, alive and well. Often ill at ease with the outspoken educated natives who represent the Third World in debates and paternalistically scornful of those who remain reserved, the dominant thus decides to weaken this term of solidarity, both by invalidating it as empowering tool and by inciting divisiveness within the Third World—a Third World within the Third World. Aggressive Third World (educated "savages") with its awareness and resistance to domination must therefore be classified apart from gentle Fourth World (uneducated "savages"). Every unaligned voice should necessarily/consequently be either a personal or a minority voice. The (impersonal) majority, as logic dictates, has to be the (aligned) dominant.

> It is, apparently, inconvenient, if not downright mind stretching [notes Alice Walker], for white women scholars to think of black women as women, perhaps because "woman" (like "man" among white males) is a name they are claiming for themselves, and themselves alone. Racism decrees that if they are now women (years ago they were ladies, but fashions change) then black women must, perforce, be something else. (While they were "ladies" black women could be "women" and so on.)[29]

Another revealing example of this separatist majority mentality is the story Walker relates of an exhibit of women painters at the Brooklyn Museum: when asked "Are there no black women painters represented here?" (none of them is, apparently), a white woman feminist simply replies "It's a *women's* exhibit!"[30] Different historical contexts, different semantic contents . . .

"Woman" and the subtle power of linguistic exclusion

What is *woman?* Long ago, during one of the forceful speeches she delivered in defense of her people, Sojourner Truth was asked by a threatened white doctor in the audience to prove to all those present that she was truly a woman:

> "There are those among us," he began in a tone characteristic of institutional training, "who question whether or not you are a woman. Some feel that maybe you are a man in a woman's disguise. To satisfy our curiosity, why don't you show your breasts to the women [sic] in this audience?"[31]

It seemed, indeed, profoundly puzzling for this man-child doctor's mind to see the Woman (or Breasts) in someone who had "never been helped into carriages, lifted over ditches, nor given the best places everywhere," who had "plowed, and planted, and gathered into barns," and who, beyond measure, triumphantly affirmed elsewhere: "Look at me! Look at my arm! . . . and no man could head me—and *ar'nt I a woman!* "[32] Definitions of *"woman," "womanhood," "femininity," "femaleness,"* and, more recently, of *"female identity"* have brought about the arrogance of such a sham anatomical curiosity—whose needs must be "satisfied"—and the legitimation of a shamelessly dehumanizing form of Indiscretion. Difference reduced to sexual identity is thus posited to justify and conceal exploitation. The Body, the most visible difference between men and women, the only one to offer a secure ground for those who seek the permanent, the feminine "nature" and "essence," remains thereby the safest basis for racist and sexist ideologies. The two merging themes of Otherness and the Identity-Body are precisely what Simone de Beauvoir discussed at length in *The Second Sex,* and continued until the time of her death to argue in the French journal she edited, *Questions Féministes.* The lead article written by the Editorial Collective under the title of "Variations on Common Themes" explains the purpose of the journal—to destroy the notion of differences between the sexes, "which gives a shape and a base to the concept of 'woman' ":

> Now, after centuries of men constantly repeating that *we* were different, here are women screaming, as if they were afraid of not being heard and as if it were an exciting discovery: "We are different!" Are you going fishing? No, I am going fishing.

The very theme of difference, whatever the differences are represented to be, is useful to the oppressing group. . . . any allegedly natural feature attributed to an oppressed group is used to imprison this group within the boundaries of a Nature which, since the group is oppressed, ideological confusion labels "nature of oppressed person" . . . to demand the right to Difference without analyzing its social character is to give back the enemy an effective weapon.[33]

Difference as the Editorial Collective of *Questions Féministes* understands and condemns it is bound to remain an integral part of naturalist ideology. It is the very kind of colonized-anthropo-logized difference the master has always happily granted his subordinates. The search and the claim for an essential female/ethnic identity-difference today can never be anything more than a move within the male-is-norm-divide-and-conquer trap. The malady lingers on. As long as words of difference serve to legitimate a discourse instead of delaying its authority to infinity, they are, to borrow an image from Audre Lorde, "noteworthy only as *decorations*." In "An Open Letter to Mary Daly," Lorde reproaches Daly (whose vision of non-European women in *Gyn/Ecology* mainly results from her insistence on universalizing women's oppression) with utilizing Lorde's words "only to testify against myself as a woman of color." She further expands this comment by specifying:

I feel you do celebrate differences between white women as a creative force towards change, rather than a reason for misunderstanding and separation. But you fail to recognize that, as women, those differences expose all women to various forms and degrees of partriarchal oppression, some of which we share, some of which we do not. . . . The oppression of women knows no ethnic nor racial boundaries, true, but that does not mean it is identical within those boundaries.

In other words,

to imply . . . that all women suffer the same oppression simply because we are women, is to lose sight of the many varied tools of patriarchy.[34]

Here you probably smile, for none of us is safe from such a critique, including I who quote Lorde in my attempts at disentangling Difference. The process of differentiation, however, continues, and speaking nearby or together with certainly differs from speaking for and about. The latter aims at the finite and dwells in the realm of fixed oppositions (subject/object difference; man/woman sexual difference), tending thereby to valorize the privileged father-daughter relationship.

Should you visit San Francisco one day, be sure to be there sometime in late January or February, for you will be witnessing one of the most spectacular festivals celebrated in America. Chinatown, which until recently was the "wickedest thoroughfare in the States," the taint of "America's dream town," a vice-ridden and overcrowded ghetto where tourists rarely venture, is now the *not-to-be-missed tourist attraction, an exotica famed for its packed restaurants, its Oriental delicacies, its glittering souvenir-crammed shops and, above all, its memorable Chinese New Year celebration. Over and over again, the (off-)scene repeats itself as if time no longer changes. How is the parade born? Where and in what circumstances was it invented? "Back home"—whose spirit this parade pretends to perpetuate—did the Chinese celebrate their New Year squeezed up along the sidewalks with several dozen hefty policemen (American and Chinese looking almost alike) on foot, on horseback, and on motor bikes (no Chinese policeman, however, has been seen on horseback or on a motor bike) to* guard *(what is supposed to be) their parade, shoo them, push them back, or call them to order if they happen to get off the line while* watching *the procession? What do you think the motives are behind such an ostentatious display of folklore, of arrogance and coercive power (besides the invariable it-is-for-your-own-good answer Order usually provides you with)? For I myself fail to see any sign of "celebration" in this segregated masquerade, where feasters are forcibly divided into actors and spectators, while participation exclusively consists in either exhibiting oneself exotically on the scene or watching the object of exhibition distantly off the scene. Chinese New Year thus takes on a typical dualistic Western face. Preserve the form of the old in the context-content of the new; this is what* decoration *means. Power arrogates to itself the right to interfere in every mass event that takes place, and the feast no longer belongs to the people, whose joint merrymaking cannot be viewed other than as a potential threat to Power. Tell me, where are those public celebrations described in tourist guides, that "spill onto every street in Chinatown and transform the squares into fairgrounds"?*

Subject-in-the-making

"In 'woman'," says Julia Kristeva, "I see something that cannot be represented, something that is not said, something above and beyond nomenclatures and ideologies."[35] Since there can be no social-political r-evolution without a r-evolution of subjects, in order to shatter the social codes, women must assume, in every (non-dualist) sense of the word, "a *negative* function: reject everything . . . definite, structured, loaded with meaning, in the existing state of society." Such a responsibility does not exclusively devolve upon women, but it is women who are in a better position to accept it, "because in social, sexual and symbolic experiences being a woman has always provided a means to another end, to becoming something else: a subject-in-the-making, a subject on trial."[36] In a book written after her visit to China, Kristeva remarks how little Chinese women differ from Chinese men—these women "whose ancestors knew better than anyone the secrets of erotic art, now so sober and so absorbed in their gray-blue suits, relaxed and austere . . . stand[ing] before their lathes or in the arms of their children . . . the 'pill' in their pockets . . .":

> One can say that they "censure the sexual difference" . . . what if this reproach, insofar as it is one, were to have no meaning except in our framework of paternal dominance, where any trace of a "central mother figure" is completely lost? What if their tradition, on condition one could strip it of its hierarchical-bureaucratic-patriarchal weight, allowed no more separation between two metaphysical entities (Men and Women); no more symbolic difference, that is, outside the biological difference, except *a subtle differentiation on both sides of the biological barrier, structured by the recognition of a social law to be assumed in order ceaselessly to be contested?* . . .
>
> If . . . one considered the family, women, and the sexual difference in the way they determine a social ethic, one could say. . . . that the basic question there is the building of a society whose active power is represented by no one . . . not even women.[37] (my italics)

The point raised by this apparent indifference to a physical distinction between men and women is not simple repression of a sexual difference, but a *different* distribution *of* sexual *difference,* therefore a challenge to the notion of (sexual) identity as commonly defined in the West and the entire gamut of concepts that ensues: femininity-femaleness-feminitude-woman-womanhood/masculinity-maleness-virility-man-manhood, and so on. In other words, sexual difference has no absolute value and is interior to the praxis of every subject. What is known as the "Phallic principle" in one part of the world (despite the dominance this part exerts over the rest) does not necessarily apply to the other parts. A thorough undermining of all power-based values would require the dismantling of the sovereign, authority-claiming subject, without which it is bound to be co-opted by power. "On a deeper level," observes Kristeva, "a woman cannot 'be'; it is something which does not even belong in the order of *being.* It follows that a feminist practice can only be negative ['our negativity is not Nietzschean anger'], at odds with what already exists so that we may say 'that's not it' and 'that's still not it.' "[38]

Ethnicity or womanhood: whose duality?

Voices of theories. Unlike Kristeva, while understanding the necessity of a "negative" feminist practice which continuously reminds us that "woman cannot be" or that we can no more speak about "woman" than about "man," I would not "try to go against metaphysical theories that censure what [she] just labeled 'a woman' " and to "dissolve identity."[39] Although these statements belong to a context of active questioning of the search for a woman's identity (and by extension, of a straight celebration of ethnic identity), they tend to invite accusations of privileging "woman" as attitude over "woman" as sex. One does not go without the other, and "woman," with its undefinable specificity (the difference, as mentioned above, both between and within entities), cannot exclusively be apprehended in relation to an apparently unsexed or supposedly beyond-the-sex "negative function." The perception of sex as a secondary attribute—a property or an adjective that one can add or subtract—to woman is a perception that still dwells in the prevailing logic of acquisition and separation. Difference understood not as an irreducible quality but as a drifting apart within "woman" articulates upon the infinity of "woman" as entities of inseparable "I's" and "Not-I's." In any case, "woman" here is not interchangeable with "man"; and to declare provocatively, as Kristeva does, that one should dissolve "even sexual identities" is, in a way, to disregard the importance of the shift that the notion of identity has undergone in woman's discourses. That shift does not lead to "a theory of female identity . . . that varies from the male model" (Gardiner), as mentioned earlier, but rather to identity as points of re-departure of the critical processes by which I have come to understand how the personal— the ethnic me, the female me—is political. Difference does not annul identity. It is beyond and alongside identity. Thus, there is simply no point outside Kristeva's "sexual identities" from which to take up a position ("When you are silent, it speaks; / When you speak, it is silent"). The same holds true for the choice many women of color feel obliged to make between ethnicity and womanhood: how can they? You never have/are one without the other. The idea of two illusorily separated identities, one ethnic, the other woman (or more precisely female), again, partakes in the Euro-American system of dualistic reasoning and its age-old divide-and-conquer tactics. Triple jeopardy means here that whenever a woman of color takes up the feminist fight, she immediately qualifies for three possible "betrayals": she can be accused of betraying either man (the "man-hater"), or her community ("people of color should stay together to fight racism"), or woman herself ("you should fight first on the women's side"). The pitting of anti-racist and anti-sexist struggles against one another allows some vocal fighters to dismiss blatantly the existence of either racism or sexism within their lines of action, as if oppression only comes in separate, monolithic forms. Thus, to understand how pervasively dominance operates via the concept of hegemony or of absent totality in plurality is to understand that the work of decolonization will have to continue within the women's movements.

Other voices of theories. Attempts have been made recently, for example, by some woman anthropologists and, more noisily, by Ivan Illich to distinguish *sex* from *gender*. The implications borne by these two notions are, indeed, far- and wide-reaching, and their differentiation certainly provide one more useful tool to inquire into this oppressor-oppressed, First World-Third World relationship. As representative terms, sex and gender point to two irreducible (although easily overlapping) systems of values, two distinct ways of perceiving the male and female dynamics. Blindness to the difference and non-interchangeability of these systems has induced the social sciences to treat native wo/men as nothing but "economic neuters" of fe/male sex. "Sex and gender," writes Illich, "are unfit to cohabit the same conceptual universe. The attempt to marry the two necessarily leads to the scientific sexism of anthropology, be it of macho or of a fem brand." Anthropology, like all the sciences of *man*, is, therefore, male-biased not only because "we who are ourselves men study men" (male investigators feed their own models to local male informants who, while rendering an account of their customs, feed them back with some native adaptations and with the best intentions, to the inquisitors from whom they first come), but also because it is gender-blind in its pretensions to science. "Its scientific logic makes it an analytical tool that studies men and women as 'anthropoi,' reduces gender to sex, and makes of a metaphorical complementarity . . . a system of two homogeneous opposites."[40] Illich's distinction between gender and sex clarifies, in many ways, the reserved attitude non-Western women maintain toward all anthropological or anthropologically reinforced feminist interpretations of their conditions. It calls attention to possibly one of the most pernicious hegemonic distortions on which nearly every anthropologist's study of the so-called sex division of labor among the "non-literate" people (and by extension, the "bi-cultural" natives) has rested: the fundamental assumption that gender is only a (primitive, underdeveloped) form of sex role.

· "By social gender," Illich specifies, "I mean the eminently local and timebound duality that sets off men and women under circumstances and conditions that prevent them from saying, doing, desiring, or perceiving 'the same thing.' By economic, or social, sex I mean the duality that stretches toward the illusory goal of economic, political, legal, or social equality between women and men." What stands out in these two definitions is the tentative exploration of a difference within duality itself. The duality Illich sees in gender and names "ambiguous," "asymmetric complementarity is *opposed* to the polarization of homogeneous characteristics that constitutes social sex" (my italics).[41] Since each culture has its own interweaving of genders, the first kind of duality remains undefinable and *is* a goal in itself. The second works toward an *objectivist* (or objectified, hense "illusory") goal and can therefore easily be determined according to a set of established criteria for equality. With such a differentiation in mind, the concept of gender may be said to be alive, open enough to deal with both differences between and differences within entities, while the concept of sex reduces the interactions between men and women to an even exchange or a mere opposition of identities. Gender as a "complementarity" is only ambiguous to the Positivistic analytical mind. In its local perspective, the gender divide is always crystal clear, even though this clarity does not result from any consistent rule that scientific reasoning may invent to salvage it and is better conveyed through myths, stories or sayings than through analyses whose necessity for order calls forth the parades of police rationalities. Thus, to simply denounce Third World women's oppression with notions and terms made to reflect or fit into Euro-American women's criteria of equality is to abide by ethnographic ideology (exposed in the previous chapter), which depends on the representation of a coherent cultural subject as source of scientific knowledge to explain a native culture and reduces every gendered activity to a sex-role stereotype. Feminism in such a context may well mean "westernization." A fundamentally "pure" (unmediated) export of or import from the dominant countries, it indirectly serves the cause of tradition upholders and provides them with a pretext for muddling all issues of oppression raised by Third World women. Standardization continues its relentless course, while Tradition remains the sacred weapon oppressors repeatedly hold up whenever the need to maintain their privileges, hence to impose the form of the old on the content of the new, arises. One can say that fear and insecurity lie behind each attempt at opposing modernism with tradition and, likewise, at setting up ethnicity against womanhood. There was a time when being a feminist meant lacking "femininity," therefore running counter to the law of womanhood; today, it is more convincing to reject feminism as a whitewashed notion and a betrayal of roots values, or vice versa, to consider the promotion of ethnic identity treacherous to that of female identity or feminism. Exchanges like the following, related by Alice Walker, are indeed very common:

> White student feminist: "But if you say that black women should work in the black community, you are saying that race comes before sex. What about black *feminists*? Should *they* be expected to work in the black community? And if so, isn't this a betrayal of their feminism? Shouldn't they work with women?"
> Our Mother [Walker's voice]: "But of course black people come in both sexes."[42]

One bounces back and forth from one extreme to another, as if races of color annul sex, as if woman can never be ethnic.

The Gender controversy

Gender, as Illich presents it, bespeaks a fundamental social polarity that varies with times and places and is never the same. It is inherent in men's and women's acts, their speeches, gestures, grasps of reality, their spaces, patterns of living, and the objects in their surroundings; it reigns in non-industrialized societies as a regulative force that renders inevitable the collective, mutual dependence of men and women, setting thereby limits to dominion, exploitation, and defeat. "Vernacular culture is a truce be-tween genders," Illich affirms, and "while under the reign of gender women might be subordinate, under *any* economic regime they are *only* the second sex."[43] However assertive, extremist, and nostalgic such a state-ment may sound, it does not, in fact, run counter to the opinions voiced by a number of Third World feminists and woman anthropologists. The latter have, for the last decade, devoted their energy to denouncing the male scholar's androcentrism, which prevents him from admitting or even recognizing the full impact of women's participation in the creation of society. They have begun challenging his limited descriptions of social reality by reinterpreting data to redefine power, influence, and status and to demonstrate that only within a male-biased perspective does the sub-jugation of women take on a universal face. Women from various Third World countries have concentrated their efforts on dispelling ideas pop-ularly held about their so-called inferior status. Such was, for example, the main intent of a group of women who gathered in Abidjan (July 3–8, 1972) to speak around the theme of "The Civilization of the Woman in African Tradition." The meeting, organized by the Society of African Culture, opened with a few statements which set the tone for the entire colloquium:

> we can only deplore the mechanism which favours the transfer to Africa of problems and their solution, of certain institutions which result from a purely Western historical process. Organizations for the promotion of women's rights. . . . tend naturally to extend identical activities into Africa, and, in so doing, to assimilate us into a strictly European mentality and historic experience.
> Hardly anything has been written about African women that has not pre-sented them as minor elements.[44]

> The African woman, at least in the precolonial society, is neither a reflection of man, nor a slave. She feels no need whatsoever to imitate him in order to express her personality.[45]

Jacqueline Ki-Zerbo emphasized the conception of *woman* as *home*. The hearth of the joint family, the needle sewing its different members together, She is *woman* in relation not only to her husband, but also to all the men of her husband's family, to her brothers, her cousins, and their friends. She is equally mother of her children and mother of all the children of the family, as well as of those belonging to her husband's friends. Thelma Awori condemned the long-lived myth of the inferiority of the African women and, in her attempts at explaining these women's conditions, raised the question of *etiquette* in social relations. Observance of the rules of etiquette, which she considered to be intrinsic to African culture, is a necessity for the survival of the community, not just an empty form with which individuals comply from mere habit. Delphine Yeyet insisted on the elevated status of women in the traditional non-state societies of Gabon. She aimed, through her speech, at destroying the myth according to which women, oppressed in primitive communes, are being liberated in today's monetary societies where men dominate. "In a subsistence economy," Yeyet observed, "men are obliged to earn their livelihood in cooperation with women without exploiting them. In a monetary economy, however, the thirst for comfort and profit pushes men to exploit women and chase them from the domains of political and social action";[46] hence, the advent, in present-day Gabon, of numerous secret and closed women's defense societies that seek to inspire respect and fear in "capitalist" men. The list of women voicing similar opinions at the colloquium is impressively long, but these three examples suffice to give an idea of the refusal of many African women to see themselves through imported words that identify them as minors with little or no rights, little or no independence, subject to the omni-authority of men. The notion of *woman* not as sexed individual but as *home*, of *etiquette* as *communal survival*, the idea of attributing women's oppression to the advent of a monetary economy, and Illich's concept of *gender* converge in many aspects. A gendered life-style implies that non-interchangeable men and women work together for the survival of their community. The contrary may be said of life under the regime of industrial economics, where genderless hands—in search of their fe/male identities—produce commodities in exchange for pay and where the law of the jungle happily prevails: Power belongs to s/he who succeeds, in the rat-(extermination)race, to consume most before(/while) being consumed.

Proceeding from one opposition to another can, however, be very limiting. It all depends on the way one renders these limits visible and succeeds in letting oppositions annul themselves by constantly annulling each other. Concepts are bound, by their linguistic nature, to yield a plural interpretation. The more this linguistic reality is taken into consideration, the less reductive prove to be the issues raised and the position adopted by the writing or speaking subject. The reign of gender Illich sets up against the regime of economic sex and the three exemplary arguments by African women mentioned above may denote a sincere effort to probe into the question of oppression, but they may also denote a form of highly reaction-

Destroying the myth according to which women, oppressed in primitive communes, are being liberated in today's monetary societies where men dominate (Stills from **NS**)

"One of these roles given to Asian women by their families and communities is to be the upholders and preservers of 'our culture.' So what happens if a woman wishes to have her own identity and wear clothes which she alone has chosen? . . . It is obvious that more than modesty is at stake" (Amrit Wilson) (Stills from I-C)

"Wounds do not seal off with humiliation. . . . So, women's condition matters little to me when the human condition is sneered at" (Stills from **SVGNN**)

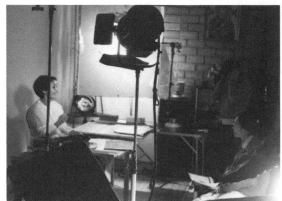

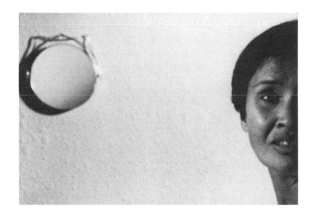

"There is the image of the woman and there is her reality. . . . They have made of us heroic workers, virtuous women. We are good mothers, good wives, heroic fighters . . . ghost women, stripped of our humanity! . . . The very idea of heroism is monstrous!" (Stills from **SVGNN**)

ary thinking rising from a deep-seated chauvinism-sexism. They may lead to a radical change in one's outlook on Third World women's struggles, as they may lead to the backwardness of "hard-core" conservatism, a conservatism that spouts out of opportunism, of the irrational fear of *losing*.[47] (Losing what? That is the question. A quick answer will run flatly as follows: losing either the master's favor or the master's position itself.) The notion of gender is pertinent to feminism as far as it denounces certain fundamental attitudes of imperialism and as long as it remains unsettled and unsettling. Illich's continual build-up of opposition between gender and sex does not, however, lead to such an opening. It tends, on the contrary, to work toward separation and enclosure. The universe in which his theories circulate—whether they relate to schooling, medical, religious, or feminist institutions—is a fixed universe with a definite contour. One can call it the uncompromising hatred of industrial economics or the cult of a subsistence-oriented mode of living; whatever the name, the aim pursued remains the same. The concept of gender is thus elaborated to fit into this perspective, hence his insistence on the irremediable *loss* of gender. Sexism postulated as a *sine qua non* of economic growth does not leave any room for gendered activities, and the two as duality are absolutely incompatible. Such a clear, irreversible division is, at times, very useful. It sheds another convincing light on the fact that sexism is no more inherent in the masculine gender (although it has been initially and predominantly practiced by men) than in the feminine gender, and when we say, for example, that the subjugation of women takes on a universal face only within a "male-biased" perspective, we are aware that we still judge this perspective in a sexist (not gendered) perspective. Recognizing one's limit and situating one's view in the realm of sexism and genderlessness certainly helps one to avoid "imputing sex to the past," reducing or distorting the realities of "native" cultures; but this does not necessarily imply that what Illich sees as a gender-bound style of perception is lost, dead, or irrecuperable. One cannot speak about the loss of a concept without at the same time knowing it can be spoken of as a gain. That vernacular speech is fading away and that industrialized language enforces the genderless perspective are borne out by Illich's own speech and writing, which, despite their careful avoidance or redefinition of key words (are bound by his own reasoning to), offer a genderless look at gender, and address a genderless *man*. Such a contradiction invites, however, further probing into the concept of gender. One wonders, indeed, whether Illich's attempts at defining gender and his persistence in dwelling on its supposed finiteness have not somehow blinded him to some of the most radical (not to be understood merely as excessive or extreme) trends in feminism today. No matter how relevant and incisive the statement may prove to be in his conceptual context, to declare that "under *any* economic regime [women] are *only* the second sex" is to oversimplify the issue. It is also willingly to ignore the importance of women's achievements in dismantling the differences within this "second-sex" as well as those between First, Second, and Third. The master is too bent on proving his point to allow for any deflection. One may say of the rigid line of his reasoning that it connotes a strong nostalgia for the past and for a purity of self-presence in life, a purity he does not hesitate to defend by crushing or crossing out all obstacles standing in his way. The place of (Illich-)the male investigator/speaker/writer remains unquestioned.

Perhaps, for those of us who have never known what life in a vernacular culture is/was and are unable to imagine what it can be/could have been, gender simply does not exist otherwise than grammatically in language. (Vernacular, as Illich uses it, denotes autonomous, non-market-related actions, or "sustenance derived from reciprocity patterns imbedded in every aspect of life, as distinguished from sustenance that comes from exchange or from vertical distribution.")[48] Attempts at reviving this notion (gender) through a genderless, industrialized language will then appear vain, for they will only be interpreted as a sophisticated—therefore most insidious—plea for a return to tradition, a tradition carried on for the benefit of men and legally (not equitably) reinforced by laws invented, brought into operation, and distorted by men for men. Such an interpretation is not totally unfounded, and there are many tradition upholders in the Third World today who would readily make use of Illich's theory of gender to back up their anti-feminist fight. Having always maintained that there should be nothing like equality and rights for women because traditionally these simply did not exist, they would turn his arguments to account and continue confidently to preach the absence of women's oppression in traditional societies. Like the Society of African Culture at the colloquium in Abidjan, they will loudly extol women's "splendid initiative, the maturity of their action," as well as their aptitude to uphold "autonomy vis-à-vis men . . . without neglecting their duties to their children or to their husbands [sic]."[49] If it is deplorable to think of women solely as sex and equal rights, it is also lamentable to see in the notion of woman-hearth-home only the cook-wife-mother whose activities should remain centered on the home despite the roles she may perform in the outside world. "The African woman today," says Simi Afonja, "is seen as intruding into realms which are exclusively for men. Hence we hear too often that the woman's place traditionally is in the home. . . . She should not therefore be found in jobs specifically meant for men."[50] When removed from its survival content, etiquette in social relations disintegrates to become mere form. Gender, reduced to a sex-determined behavior, serves to promote inequal-

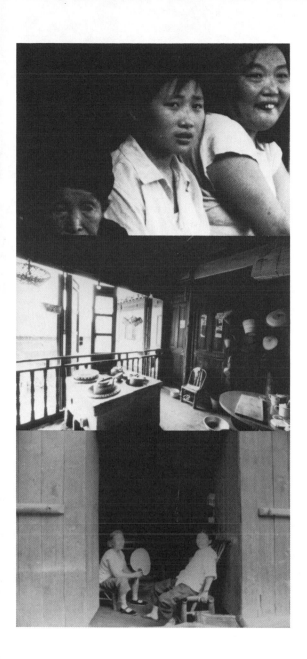

The re-writing of what is private and what is public, the reversal and displacement of the two realms and their opposition (Stills from **I-C**)

ity in a system of production, exchange, and consumption where "the woman," according to Jeanne Nzaou-Mabika, "has little opportunity to take the initiative and to exercise her creative ability. The least manifestations of a desire for change in ancient practices is regarded as an intolerable rebellion."[51] Here, Illich's theory shows, again, that distinctions need to be made both (1) between the transgression or infraction of gender in a gendered society and the deviation from a sex-determined behavior in a society where gender has disappeared and (2) between gender infringement and the fading of the gender line itself. Violations of the gender divide, which have occurred in all times and places, mostly result from technological discovery, public calamity, private misfortune, or occasional emergencies. Having always been experienced as a terrifying force when carried out collectively, they also constitute an effective means of redressing a power imbalance or defying the established order, and they aim, not at effacing the gender line, but at *confirming it through change*. Gender thus understood approximates Julia Kristeva's earlier definition of that which characterizes the relation between women and men in China: "a subtle differentiation on both sides of the biological barrier, structured by the recognition of a social law to be assumed in order ceaselessly to be contested." A social regulator and a political potential for change, gender, in its own way, baffles definition. It escapes the "*diagnostic* power" of a sex-oriented language/sex-identified logic and coincides thereby with *difference*, whose inseparable temporal and spatial dynamics produces the illusion of identity while undermining it relentlessly. In today's context, to defend a gendered way of living is to fight for difference, a difference that postpones to infinity and subverts the trend toward unisex behavioral patterns. The story of gender-as-difference is, therefore, not "the story of what has been lost" (Illich), but the story of that which does not readily lend itself to (demonstrative) narrations or descriptions and continues to mutate with/beyond nomenclature.

"Reassemblage. From silences to silences, the fragile essence of each fragment sparks across the screen, subsides, and takes flight. Almost there half named" (Stills from **R**)

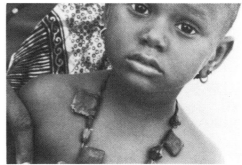

IV

Grandma's Story

See all things howsoever they flourish
Return to the root from which they grew
This return to the root is called Quietness
—Lao Tzu, *Tao-te-ching*, 16 (tr. A. Waley)

Truth and fact: story and history

Let me tell you a story. For all I have is a story. Story passed on from generation to generation, named Joy. Told for the joy it gives the storyteller and the listener. Joy inherent in the process of storytelling. Whoever understands it also understands that a story, as distressing as it can be in its joy, never takes anything away from anybody. Its name, remember, is Joy. Its double, Woe Morrow Show.

> Let the one who is diseuse, one who is mother who waits nine days and nine nights be found. Restore memory. Let the one who is diseuse, one who is daughter restore spring with her each appearance from beneath the earth. The ink spills thickest before it runs dry before it stops writing at all. (Theresa Hak Kyung Cha)[1]

Something must be said. Must be said that has not been *and* has been said before. "It will take a long time, but the story must be told. There must not be any lies" (Leslie Marmon Silko). It will take a long time for living cannot be told, not merely told: living is not livable. Understanding, however, is creating, and living, such an immense gift that thousands of people benefit from each past or present life being lived. The story depends upon every one of us to come into being. It needs us all, needs our remembering, understanding, and creating what we have heard together to keep on coming into being. The story of a people. Of us, peoples. Story, history, literature (or religion, philosophy, natural science, ethics)—all in one. They call it the tool of primitive man, the simplest vehicle of truth. When history separated itself from story, it started indulging in accumulation and facts. Or it thought it could. It thought it could build up to History because the

Past, unrelated to the Present and the Future, is lying there in its entirety, waiting to be revealed and related. The act of revealing bears in itself a magical (not factual) quality—inherited undoubtedly from "primitive" storytelling—for the Past perceived as such is a well-organized past whose organization is already given. Managing to identify with History, history (with a small letter h) thus manages to oppose the factual to the fictional (turning a blind eye to the "magicality" of its claims); the story-writer—the historian—to the story-teller. As long as the transformation, manipulations, or redistributions inherent in the collecting of events are overlooked, the division continues its course, as sure of its itinerary as it certainly dreams to be. Story-writing becomes history-writing, and history quickly sets itself apart, consigning story to the realm of tale, legend, myth, fiction, literature. Then, since fictional and factual have come to a point where they mutually exclude each other, fiction, not infrequently, means lies, and fact, truth. DID IT REALLY HAPPEN? IS IT A TRUE STORY?

> I don't want to listen to any more of your stories [Maxine Hong Kingston screamed at her champion-story-talker mother]; they have no logic. They scramble me up. You lie with stories. You won't tell me a story and then say, "This is a true story," or "This is just a story." I can't tell the difference. I don't even know what your real names are. I can't tell what's real and what you made up.[2]

Which truth? the question unavoidably arises. The story has been defined as "a free narration, not necessarily factual but truthful in character. . . . [It] gives us human nature in its bold outlines; history, in its individual details."[3] Truth. Not one but two: truth and fact, just like in the old times when queens were born and kings were made in Egypt. (Queens and princesses were then "Royal Mothers" from birth, whereas the king wore the crown of high priest and did not receive the Horus-name until his coronation.) Poetry, Aristotle said, is truer than history. Storytelling as literature (narrative poetry) must then be truer than history. If we rely on history to tell us what happened at a specific time and place, we can rely on the story to tell us not only what might have happened, but also what is happening at an unspecified time and place. No wonder that in old tales storytellers are very often women, witches, and prophets. The African griot and griotte are well known for being poet, storyteller, historian, musician, and magician—all at once. But why truth at all? Why this battle for truth and on behalf of truth? I do not remember having asked grand mother once whether the story she was telling me was true or not. Neither do I recall her asking me whether the story I was reading her was true or not. We knew we could make each other cry, laugh, or fear, but we never thought of saying to each other, "This is just a story." A story is a story. There was no need for clarification—a need many adults considered "natural" or imperative among children—for there was no such thing as "a blind acceptance of the story as literally true." Perhaps the story has become *just* a story when I have become adept at consuming truth as fact. Imagination is thus equated with falsification, and I am made to believe that if, accordingly, I am not told or do not establish in so many words what is true and what is false, I or the listener may no longer be able to differentiate fancy from fact (sic). Literature and history once were/still are stories: this does not necessarily mean that the space they form is undifferentiated, but that this space can articulate on a different set of principles, one which may be said to stand outside the hierarchical realm of facts. On the one hand, each society has its own politics of truth; on the other hand, being truthful is being in the in-between of all regimes of truth. Outside specific time, outside specialized space: "Truth embraces with it all other abstentions other than itself" (T. Hak Kyung Cha).

Keepers and transmitters

Truth is when it is itself no longer. Diseuse, Thought-Woman, Spider-Woman, griotte, storytalker, fortune-teller, witch. If you have the patience to listen, she will take delight in relating it to you. An entire history, an entire vision of the world, a lifetime story. Mother always has a mother. And Great Mothers are recalled as the goddesses of all waters, the sources of diseases and of healing, the protectresses of women and of childbearing. To listen carefully is to preserve. But to preserve is to burn, for understanding means creating.

> Let the one who is diseuse, Diseuse de bonne aventure. Let her call forth.
> Let her break open the spell cast upon time upon time again and again. (T.
> Hak Kyung Cha)[4]

The world's earliest archives or libraries were the memories of women. Patiently transmitted from mouth to ear, body to body, hand to hand. In the process of storytelling, speaking and listening refer to realities that do not involve just the imagination. The speech is seen, heard, smelled, tasted, and touched. It destroys, brings into life, nurtures. Every woman partakes in the chain of guardianship and of transmission. In Africa it is said that every griotte who dies is a whole library that burns down (a "library in which the archives are not classified but are completely inventoried" [A. Hampate Ba]). Phrases like "I sucked it at my mother's breast" or "I have it from Our Mother" to express what has been passed down by the elders are common in this part of the world. Tell me and let me tell my hearers what I have heard from you who heard it from your mother and your grandmother, so that what is said may be guarded and unfailingly transmitted to the women of tomorrow, who will be our children and the children of our children. These are the opening lines she used to chant before embarking on a story. I owe that to you, her and her, who owe it to her, her and her. I memorize, recognize, and name my source(s), not to validate my voice through the voice of an authority (for we, women, have little authority in the History of Literature, and wise women never draw their powers from authority), but to evoke her and sing. The bond between women and word. Among women themselves. To produce their full effect, words must, indeed, be chanted rhythmically, in cadences, off cadences.

> My great-grandmama told my grandmama the part she lived through that my grandmama didn't live through and my grandmama told my mama what they both lived through and my mama told me what they all lived through and we were supposed to pass it down like that from generation to generation so we'd never forget. Even though they'd burned everything to play like it didn't ever happen. (Gayl Jones)[5]

In this chain and continuum, I am but one link. The story is me, neither me nor mine. It does not really belong to me, and while I feel greatly responsible for it, I also enjoy the irresponsibility of the pleasure obtained through the process of transferring. Pleasure in the copy, pleasure in the reproduction. No repetition can ever be identical, but my story carries with it their stories, their history, and our story repeats itself endlessly despite our persistence in denying it. *I don't believe it. That story could not happen today.* Then someday our children will speak about us here present, about those days when things like that could happen . . . :

> It was like I didn't know how much was me and Mutt and how much was Great Gram and Corregidora—like Mama when she had started talking like Great Gram. But was what Corregidora had done to *her*, to *them*, any worse than what Mutt had done to me, than what we had done to each other, than what Mama had done to Daddy, or what he had done to her in return. . . . (Gayl Jones)[6]

> Upon seeing her you know how it was for her. You know how it might have been. You recline, you lapse, you fall, you see before you what you have seen before. Repeated, without your even knowing it. It is you standing there. It is you waiting outside in the summer day. (T. Hak Kyung Cha)[7]

Every gesture, every word involves our past, present, and future. The body never stops accumulating, and years and years have gone by mine without my being able to stop them, stop it. My sympathies and grudges appear at the same time familiar and unfamiliar to me; I dwell in them, they dwell in me, and we dwell in each other, more as guest than as owner. My story, no doubt, is me, but it is also, no doubt, older than me. Younger than me, older than the humanized. Unmeasurable, uncontainable, so immense that it exceeds all attempts at humanizing. But humanizing we do, and also overdo, for the vision of a story that has no end—no end, no middle, no beginning; no start, no stop, no progression; neither backward nor forward, only a stream that flows into another stream, an open sea—is the vision of a madwoman. "The unleashed tides of muteness," as Clarice Lispector puts it. We fear heights, we fear the headless, the bottomless, the boundless. And we are in terror of letting ourselves be engulfed by the depths of muteness. This is why we keep on doing violence to words: to tame and cook the wild-raw, to adopt the vertiginously infinite. Truth does not make sense; it exceeds meaning and exceeds measure. It exceeds all regimes of truth. So, when we insist on telling over and over again, we insist on repetition in re-creation (and vice versa). On distributing the story into smaller proportions that will correspond to the capacity of absorption of our mouths, the capacity of vision of our eyes, and the capacity of bearing of our bodies. Each story is at once a fragment and a whole; a whole within a whole. And the same story has always been changing, for things which do not shift and grow cannot continue to circulate. Dead. Dead times, dead words, dead tongues. Not to repeat in oblivion.

> Sediment. Turned stone. Let the one who is diseuse dust breathe away the distance of the well. Let the one who is diseuse again sit upon the stone nine days and nine nights. thus. Making stand again, Eleusis. (T. Hak Kyung Cha)[8]

Storytelling in the "civilized" context

The simplest vehicle of truth, the story is also said to be "a phase of communication," "the natural form for revealing life." Its fascination may be explained by its power both to give a vividly felt insight into the life of other people and to revive or keep alive the forgotten, dead-ended, turned-into-stone parts of ourselves. To the wo/man of the West who spends time recording and arranging the "data" concerning storytelling as well as "the many rules and taboos connected with it," this tool of primitive wo/man has provided primitive peoples with opportunities "to train their speech, formulate opinions, and express themselves" (Anna Birgitta Rooth). It gives "a sympathetic understanding of their limitations in knowledge, and an appreciation of our privileges in civilization, due largely to the struggles of the past" (Clark W. Hetherington). It informs of the explanations they invented for "the things [they] did not understand," and represents their religion, "a religion growing out of fear of the unknown" (Katherine Dunlap Cather). In summary, the story is either a mere practice of the art of rhetoric or "a repository of obsolete customs" (A. Skinner). It is mainly valued for its artistic potential and for the "religious beliefs" or "primitive-mind"-revealing superstitions mirrored by its content. (Like the supernatural, is the superstitious another product of the Western mind? For to accept even temporarily Cather's view on primitive religion, one is bound to ask: which [institutionalized] religion does not grow out of fear of the unknown?) Associated with backwardness, ignorance, and illiteracy, storytelling in the more "civilized" context is therefore relegated to the realm of children. "The fact that the story is the product of primitive man," wrote Herman H. Horne, "explains in part why the children hunger so for the story."[9] "Wherever there is no written language, wherever the people are too unlettered to read what is written," Cather equally remarked, "they still believe the legends. They love to hear them told and retold. . . . As it is with unlettered peasants today, as it was with tribesmen in primitive times and with the great in medieval castle halls, it still is with the child."[10] Primitive means elementary, therefore infantile. No wonder then that in the West storytelling is treasured above all for its educational force in the kindergarten and primary school. The mission of the storyteller, we thus hear, is to "teach children the tales their *fathers* knew," to mold ideals, and to "illuminate facts." For children to gain "right feelings" and to "think true," the story as a pedagogical tool must inform so as to keep their opinion "abreast of the scientific truth of the time, instead of dragging along in the superstitions of the past." But for the story to be well-told information, it must be related "in as fascinating a form as [in] the old myths and fables."[11] Patch up the content of the new and the form of the old, or impose one on the other. The dis-ease lingers on. With (traditional but non-superstitious?) formulas like "once upon a time" and "long, long ago," the storyteller can be reasonably sure of making "a good beginning." For many people truth has the connotation of uniformity and prescription. Thinking true means thinking in conformity with a certain scientific (read "scientistic") discourse produced by certain institutions. Not only has the "civilized" mind classified many of the realities it *does not understand* in the categories of the untrue and the superstitious, it has also turned the story—as total event of a community, a people—into a *fatherly* lesson for children of a certain age. Indeed, in the "civilized" context, only children are allowed to indulge in the so-called fantastic or the fantastic-true. They are perceived as belonging to a world apart, one which adults (compassionately) control and populate with toys—that is to say, with false human beings (dolls), false animals, false objects (imitative, diminutive versions of the "real"). "Civilized" adults fabricate, structure, and segregate the children's world; they invent toys for the latter to *play* with and stories of a specially adapted, more digestive kind to absorb, yet they insist on molding this world according to the scientifically true—the real, obviously not in its full scale, but in a reduced scale: that which is supposed to be the (God-like-) child's scale. Stories, especially "primitive-why stories" or fairy tales, must be carefully sorted and graded, for children should neither be "deceived" nor "duped" and "there should never be any doubt in [their] mind as to what is make-believe and what is real." In other words, the difference "civilized" adults recognize in the little people's world is a mere matter of scale. The forms of constraint that rule these bigger people's world and allow them to distinguish with certainty the false from the true must, unquestionably, be exactly the same as the ones that regulate the smaller people's world. The apartheid type of difference continues to operate in all spheres of "civilized" life. There does not seem to be any possibility either as to the existence of such things as, for example, two (or more) different realms of make-believe or two (or more) different realms of truth. The "civilized" mind is an indisputably clear-cut mind. If once upon a time people believed in the story and thought it was true, then why should it be false today? If true and false keep on changing with the times, then isn't it true that what is "crooked thinking" today may be "right thinking" tomorrow? What kind of people, we then wonder, walk around asking obstinately: "Is there not danger of making liars of children by feeding them on these [fairy] stories?" What kind of people set out for northern Alaska to study storytelling among the Indians and come round to writing: "What especially impressed me was their eagerness to make me understand. To me this eagerness became a proof of the high value they set on their stories and what they represented"?[12] What kind of people, indeed, other than the very kind for whom the story is "*just* a story"?

A regenerating force

An oracle and a bringer of joy, the storyteller is the living memory of her time, her people. She composes on life but does not lie, for composing is not imagining, fancying, or inventing. When asked, "What is oral tradition?" an African "traditionalist" (a term African scholars consider more accurate than the French term "griot" or "griotte," which tends to confuse traditionalists with mere public entertainers) would most likely be non-plussed. As A. Hampate Ba remarks, "[s/he] might reply, after a lengthy silence: 'It is total knowledge,' and say no more."[13] She might or might not reply so, for what is called here "total knowledge" is not really nameable. At least it cannot be named (so) without incurring the risk of sliding right back into one of the many slots the "civilized" discourse of knowledge readily provides it with. The question "What is oral tradition?" is a question-answer that needs no answer at all. Let the one who is civilized, the one who invents "oral tradition," let him define it for himself. For "oral" and "written" or "written" versus "oral" are notions that have been as heavily invested as the notions of "true" and "false" have always been. (If writing, as mentioned earlier, does not express language but encompasses it, then where does the written stop? The line distinguishing societies with writing from those without writing seems most ill-defined and leaves much to be desired . . .) Living is neither oral nor written—how can the living and the lived be contained in the merely oral? Furthermore, when she composes on life she not only gives information, entertains, develops, or expands the imagination. Not only educates. Only practices a craft. "Mind breathes mind," a civilized man wrote, "power feels power, and absorbs it, as it were. The telling of stories refreshes the mind as a bath refreshes the body; it gives exercise to the intellect and its powers; it tests the judgment and the feelings."[14] Man's view is always reduced to man's mind. For this is the part of himself he values most. THE MIND. The intellect and its powers. Storytelling allows the "civilized" narrator above all to renew his mind and exercise power through his intellect. Even though the motto reads "Think, act, and feel," his task, he believes, is to ease the passage of the story from mind to mind. She, however, who sets out to revive the forgotten, to survive and supersede it ("From stone. Layers. Of stone upon stone between the layers, dormant. No more" [T. Hak Kyung Cha].[15]), she never speaks of and cannot be content with mere matters of the mind—such as mind transmission. The storyteller has long been known as a personage of power. True, she partakes in this living heritage of power. But her powers do more than illuminate or refresh the mind. They extinguish as quickly as they set fire. They wound as easily as they soothe. And not necessarily the mind. Abraham Lincoln, accurately observed that "the sharpness of a refusal, or the edge of a rebuke, may be blunted by an appropriate story, so as to save wounded feeling and yet serve the purpose . . . story-telling as an emollient saves me much friction and distress."[16] Yet this is but one more among the countless functions of storytelling. Humidity, receptivity, fecundity. Again, her speech is seen, heard, smelled, tasted, and touched. Great Mother is the goddess of all waters, the protectress of women and of childbearing, the unweary sentient hearer, the healer and also the bringer of diseases. She who gives always accepts, she who wishes to preserve never fails to refresh. Regenerate.

She was already in her mid-sixties
when I discovered that she would listen to me
to all my questions and speculations.
I was only seven or eight years old then. (Leslie Marmon Silko)[17]

Salivate, secrete the words. No water, no birth, no death, no life. No speech, no song, no story, no force, no power. The entire being is engaged in the act of speaking-listening-weaving-procreating. If she does not cry she will turn into stone. Utter, weep, wet, let it flow so as to break through (it). Layers of stone amidst layers of stone. Break with her own words. The interrelation of woman, water, and word pervades African cosmogonies. Among the Dogon, for example, the process of regeneration which the eight ancestors of the Dogon people had to undergo was carried out in the waters of the womb of the female Nummo (the Nummo spirits form a male and female Pair whose essence is divine) *while she spoke* to herself and to her own sex, accompanied by the male Nummo's voice. "The spoken Word entered into her and wound itself round her womb in a spiral of eight turns . . . the spiral of the Word gave to the womb its regenerative movement." Of the fertilizing power of words and their transmissions through women, it is further said that:

> the first Word had been pronounced [read "scanned"] in front of the genitalia of a woman. . . . The Word finally came from the ant-hill, that is, from the mouth of the seventh Nummo [the seventh ancestor and master of speech], which is to say from a woman's genitalia.
> The Second Word, contained in the craft of weaving, emerged from a mouth, which was also the primordial sex organ, in which the first childbirths took place.[18]

Thus, as a wise Dogon elder (Ogotemmêli) pointed out, "issuing from a woman's sexual part, the Word enters another sexual part, namely the ear." (The ear is considered to be bisexual, the auricle being male and the auditory aperture, female.) From the ear, it will, continuing the cycle, go to the sexual part where it encircles the womb. African traditions conceive of speech as a gift of God/dess and a force of creation. In Fulfulde, the word for "speech" (*haala*) has the connotation of "giving strength," and by extension of "making material." Speech is the materialization, externalization, and internalization of the vibrations of forces. That is why, A. Hampate Ba noted, "every manifestation of a force in any form whatever is to be regarded as its speech . . . everything in the universe speaks. . . . If speech is strength, that is because it creates a *bond of coming-and-going* which generates *movement and rhythm* and therefore *life and action* [my italics]. This movement to and fro is symbolized by the weaver's feet going up and down . . . (the symbolism of the loom is entirely based on creative speech in action)."[19] Making material: spinning and weaving is a euphonious heritage of wo/mankind handed on from generation to generation of weavers within the clapping of the shuttle and the creaking of the block—which the Dogon call "the creaking of the Word." "The cloth was the Word"; the same term, *soy*, is used among the Dogon to signify both the woven material and the spoken word. Life is a perpetual to and fro, a dis/continuous releasing and absorbing of the self. Let her weave her story within their stories, her life amidst their lives. And while she weaves, let her whip, spur, and set them on fire. Thus making them sing again. Very softly a-new a-gain.

At once "black" and "white" magic

"The witch is a woman; the wizard is a male imitation" (Robert Briffault). In many parts of the world, magic (and witchcraft) is regarded as essentially a woman's function. It is said that "in primitive thought every woman is credited with the possession of magic powers." Yet she who possesses that power is always the last one to credit it. Old Lao Tzu warned: the wo/man of virtue is not virtuous; the one who never fails in virtue has no virtue at all. Practicing power for the sake of power—an idea implied in the widely assumed image of the witch as exclusively an evil-doer—is an inheritance, I suspect, of the "civilized" mind. She who brings death and disease also brings life and health. The line dividing the good and the evil, magic and witchcraft, does not always seem to be as clear-cut as it should be. In the southern Celebes, for example, "All the deities and spirits from whom sorcerers, whether male or female, derive their power are spoken of as their 'grandmothers.' " Throughout Africa, priestesses are called "Mothers," and the numerous female fetishes served exclusively by women are known as the "Mother fetishes." Among the Butwa, the female hierophants are named "the mothers of the Butwa mysteries." Among the Bir, the women are those who perform the essential ritual of maintaining the sacred fire. In Indonesia, America, northern Asia, and northern Europe, it has been demonstrated that "magical practices and primitive priestly functions formerly belonged to the exclusive sphere of women and that they were taken up [appropriated] by men at a comparatively late epoch." Thus, the adoption of female attire by male shamans and priests is a widespread phenomenon that still prevails in today's religious contexts. Imitating women and wearing women's clothes—priestly robes, skirts, aprons, sottanas, woven loinclothes—are regarded as bestowing greater power: the Mothers' power.[20] Of making material. Of composing on life. Her speech, her storytelling is at once magic, sorcery, and religion. It enchants. It animates, sets into motion, and rouses the forces that lie dormant in things, in beings. It is "bewitching." At once "black" and "white" magic. Which, however, causes sickness and death? which brings joy into life? For white, remember, is the color for mourning in many cultures. The same "medicines," the same dances, the same sorcery are said to be used in both. As occasion arises, the same magic may serve for beneficent *and* maleficent ends. This is why her power is so dreaded; because it can be used for harm; because when it is wielded by one sex, it arouses alarm in the other. The (wizard's) game dates from the times when every practice of this art by women became a threat to men and was automatically presumed to be malignant in intention; when every magic woman must necessarily be a witch—no longer a fairy who works wonders nor a Mother-priestess-prophetess who nurtures, protects, restores, and warns against ill-will. Ill assumption leads to ill action. Men appropriate women's power of "making material" to themselves and, not infrequently, corrupt it out of ignorance. The story becomes *just a* story. It becomes a good or bad lie. And in the more "civilized" contexts where women are replaced and excluded from magico-religious functions, adults who still live on storytelling become bums who spend their time feeding on lies, "them big old lies we tell when we're jus' sittin' around here on the store porch doin' nothin'." When Zora Neale Hurston came back to Eatonville, Florida, to collect old stories, her home folks proudly told her: "Zora, you come to de right place if lies is what you want. Ah'm gointer lie up a nation"; or "Now, you gointer hear lies above suspicion"; or else "We kin tell you some lies most any ole time. We never run outer lies and lovin'."[21] All right, let them call it lie, let us smile and call it lie too if that satisfies them, but "let de lyin' go on!" For we do not *just* lie, we lie and love, we "lie up a nation," and our lies are "above suspicion." How can they be otherwise when they derive their essence from that gift of God: speech? Speech, that active agent in our Mothers' magic; speech, which owes its fertilizing power to . . . who else but the Mother of God?

The woman warrior: she who breaks open the spell

"Thought-Woman / is sitting in her room / and whatever she thinks about / appears. / She thought of her sisters, / . . . / and together they

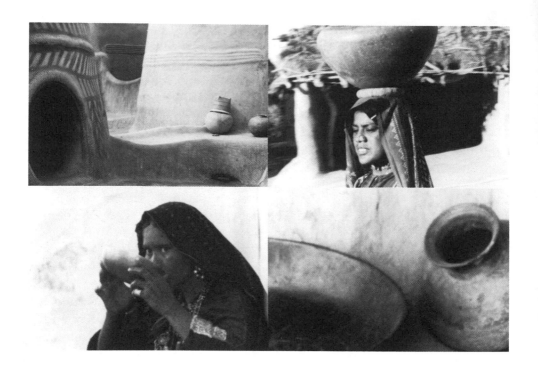

From Africa to India and vice versa. Every woman partakes in the chain of guardianship and of transmission. Every griotte who dies is a whole library that burns down (Photo of Nankani house and stills from **I-C**)

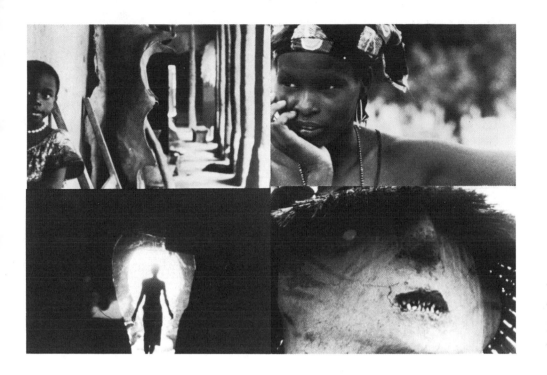

We fear heights, we fear the headless, the bottomless, and the boundless. . . . This is why we keep on doing violence to words: to tame and cook the wild raw, to adopt the vertiginously infinite (Stills from **NS**)

created the Universe / . . . / Thought-Woman, the spider, / named things
and / as she named them / they appeared (Leslie Marmon Silko).[22] The
touch infinitely delicate awakens, restores them to life, letting them surge
forth in their own measures and their own rhythms. The touch infinitely
attentive of a fairy's wand, a woman's voice, or a woman's hand, which
goes to meet things in the dark and pass them on without deafening,
without extinguishing in the process. Intense but gentle, it holds words
out in the direction of things or lays them down nearby things so as to call
them and breathe new life into them. Not to capture, to chain them up, nor
to mean. Not to instruct nor to discipline. But to kindle that zeal which
hibernates within each one of us. "Speech may create peace, as it may
destroy it. It is like fire," wrote A. Hampate Ba, "One ill-advised word may
start a war just as one blazing twig may touch off a great conflagration. . . .
Tradition, then, confers on . . . the Word not only creative power but a
double function of saving and destroying."[23] Her words are like fire. They
burn and they destroy. It is, however, only by burning that they lighten.
Destroying and saving, therefore, are here one single process. Not two
processes posed in opposition or in conflict. They would like to order
everything around hierarchical oppositions. They would like to cut her
power into endless opposing halves or cut herself from the Mothers'
powers—setting her against either her mother, her godmother, her
mother-in-law, her grandmother, her daughter, or her granddaughter.
One of them has to be wicked so as to break the network of transmission.
This is cleverly called jealousy among women, the jealousy of the woman
who cannot suffer seeing her daughter or another woman take more
pleasure in life than herself. For years and years, centuries and centuries,
they have devoted their energies to breaking bonds and spreading discords
and confusion. Divide and conquer. Mothers fighting mothers. Here is
what an Indian witch has to say on "white skin people / like the belly of a
fish / covered with hair":

. . . . They see no life
When they look
they see only objects.
. . . . They fear
They fear the world.
They destroy what they fear.
They fear themselves.
. . . . Stolen rivers and mountains
the stolen land will eat their hearts
and jerk their mouths from the Mother.
The people will starve.[24]

These are excerpts of a story passed on by Leslie Marmon Silko. The story
is the vision of a witch who, a long time ago, at a contest of witches from all

the pueblos, "didn't show off any dark thunder charcoals or red anthill beads" like the other witches, but only asked them to listen: "What I have is a story. . . . laugh if you want to / but as I tell the story / it will begin to happen." Scanned by the refrain "set in motion now / set in motion / to work for us" the story thus unfolds, naming as it proceeds the killing, the destruction, the foul deed, the loss of the white man, and with it, the doom of the Indian people. "It isn't so funny. . . . Take it back. Call that story back," said the audience by the end of the story, but the witch answered: "It's already turned loose / It's already coming. / It can't be called back." A story is *not* just a story. Once the forces have been aroused and set into motion, they can't simply be stopped at someone's request. Once told, the story is bound to circulate; humanized, it may have a temporary end, but its effects linger on and its end is never truly an end. Who among us has not, to a certain extent, felt what George Ebers, for example, felt toward his mother's stories: "When the time of rising came, I climbed joyfully into my mother's warm bed, and never did I listen to more beautiful fairy tales than at those hours. They became instinct with life to me and have always remained so. . . . It is a singular thing that actual events which happened in those early days have largely vanished from my memory, but the fairy tales I heard and secretly experienced became firmly impressed on my mind."[25] The young beautiful fairy and the old ugly witch, remember, have the same creative power, the same decisive force of speech. As she names them, they appear . . . The story tells us not only what might have happened, but also what *is happening* at an unspecified time and place. Whenever Ebers had the slightest doubt in mind, he would immediately appeal to his mother, for he thought "she could never be mistaken and knew that she always told the truth." Lying is not a mother's attribute. Or else, if lying is what you think she does, then she will "never run outer lies and lovin'."

> When we Chinese girls listened to the adult talk-story, we learned that we failed if we grew up to be but wives or slaves. We could be heroines, swordswomen. . . . Night after night my mother would talk-story until we fell asleep. I couldn't tell where the stories left off and the dreams began, her voice the voice of the heroines in my sleep. . . . At last I saw that I too had been in the presence of great power, my mother talking-story. . . . She said I would grow up a wife and a slave, but she taught me the song of the warrior woman, Fa Mu Lan. I would have to grow up a warrior woman. (Maxine Hong Kingston)[26]

She fires her to achievement and she fires her with desire to emulate. She fires her with desire to emulate the heroines of whom she told and she fires her with desire to emulate the heroine who tells of the other heroines, "I too had been in the presence of great power, my mother talking-story."

What is transmitted from generation to generation is not only the stories, but the very power of transmission. The stories are highly inspiring, and so is she, the untiring storyteller. She, who suffocates the codes of lie and truth. She, who loves to tell and retell and loves to hear them told and retold night after night again and again. Hong Kingston grows up a warrior woman and a warrior-woman-storyteller herself. She is the woman warrior who continues to fight in America the fight her mothers fought in China. Even though she is often "mad at the Chinese for lying so much," and blames her mother for lying with stories, she happily *lets the lying go on* by retelling us her mother's "lies" and offering us versions of her stories that can be called lies themselves. Her brother's version of a story, she admits it herself, "may be better than mine because of its bareness, not twisted into designs." Her brother, indeed, is no woman warrior-storyteller. Hong Kingston's apparent confusion of story and reality is, in fact, no confusion at all since it is an unending one; her parents often accuse her of not being able to "tell a joke from real life" and to understand that Chinese "like to say the opposite." Even the events described by her relatives in their letters from China she finds suspect: "I'd like to go to China and see those people and find out what's cheat story and what's not." The confusion she experienced in her girlhood is the confusion we all experience in life, even when we think, as adults, that we have come up with definite criteria for the true and the false. What is true and what is not, and who decides so if we wish not to have this decision made *for* us? When, for example, Hong Kingston yells at her mother: "You can't stop me from talking. You tried to cut off my tongue, but it didn't work," we not only know she is quite capable of telling "fancy" from "facts," we are also carried a step further in this differentiation by her mother's answer: "I cut it to make you talk more, not less, you dummy."[27] (Her mother has already affirmed elsewhere that she cut it so that her daughter would not be "tongue-tied.") The opening story of *The Woman Warrior* is a forbidden story ("No Name woman") that begins with Hong Kingston's mother saying: "You must not tell anyone what I am about to tell you." Twenty years after she heard this story about her father's sister who drowned herself and her baby in the family well, not only has Hong Kingston broken open the spell cast upon her aunt by retelling the story—"I alone devote pages of paper to her"—but she has done it in such a way as to reach thousands and thousands of listeners and readers. Tell it to the world. To preserve is to pass on, not to keep for oneself. A story told is a story bound to circulate. By telling her daughter not to tell it to anyone, the mother knew what she was supposed to say, for "That's what Chinese say. We like to say the opposite." She knew she was in fact the first before her daughter to break open the spell. The family cursed her, she who committed adultery and was such a spite suicide (the aunt); the men (her brothers) tabooed her name and went on living "as if she had never been born"; but the women (Hong Kingston's mother and those who partook in this aunt's death) would have to carry her with(in) them for life and pass her on, even though they condemned her no less. For every woman is the woman of all women, and this one died first and foremost for being a woman. ("Now that you have started to menstruate," the mother warned her daughter, "what happened to her could happen to you. Don't humiliate us.") Hong Kingston has, in her own way, retained many of the principles of her mother's storytelling. If, in composing with "fancy" and "fact," the latter knows when she should say "white is white" and when she should say "white is black" in referring to the same thing, her daughter also knows when to dot her i's and when not to. Her writing, neither fiction nor non-fiction, constantly invites the reader either to drift naturally from the realm of imagination to that of actuality or to live them both without ever being able to draw a clear line between them yet never losing sight of their differentiation. What Hong Kingston does *not* tell us about her mother but allows us to read between the lines and in the gaps of her stories reveals as much about her mother as what she *does* tell us about her. This, I feel, is the most "truthful" aspect of her work, the very power of her storytelling. *The Woman Warrior* ends with a story Hong Kingston's mother told her, not when she was young, she says, "but recently, when I told her I also talk-story." The beginning of the story, which relates how the family in China came to love the theater through the grandmother's passion for it and her generosity, is the making of the mother. The ending of the story, which recalls one of the songs the poetess Ts'ai Yen composed while she was a captive of the barbarians and how it has been passed down to the Chinese, is the making of the daughter—Hong Kingston herself. Two powerful woman storytellers meet at the end of the book, both working at strengthening the ties among women while commemorating and transmitting the powers of our foremothers. At once a grandmother, a poetess, a storyteller, and a woman warrior.

A cure and a protection from illness

I grew up with storytelling. My earliest memories are of my grandmother telling me stories while she watered the morning-glories in her yard. Her stories were about incidents from long ago, incidents which occurred before she was born but which she told as certainly as if she had been there. The chanting or telling of ancient stories to effect certain cures or protect from illness and harm have always been part of the Pueblo's curing ceremonies. I feel the power that the stories still have to bring us together, especially when there is loss and grief. (Leslie Marmon Silko)[28]

Refresh, regenerate, or purify. Telling stories and watering morning-glories both function to the same effect. For years and years she has been renewing her forces with regularity to keep them intact. Such ritual ablutions—the telling and retelling—allow her to recall the incidents that occurred before she was born with as much certainty as if she had witnessed them herself. The words passed down from mouth to ear (one sexual part to another sexual part), womb to womb, body to body are the remembered ones. S/He whose belly cannot contain (also read "retain") words, says a Malinke song, will succeed at nothing. The further they move away from the belly, the more liable they are to be corrupted. (Words that come from the MIND and are passed on directly "from mind to mind" are, consequently, highly suspect . . .) In many parts of Africa, the word "belly" refers to the notion of occult power. Among the Basaa of Cameroon, for example, the term *hu*, meaning (a human being's) "stomach," is used to designate "a thing whose origin and nature nobody knows," but which is unanimously attributed to women and their powers. A Basaa man said he heard from his fathers that "it was the woman who introduced the *hu*" into human life. In several myths of the Basaa's neighboring peoples, *evu*, the equivalent of the Basaa's *hu*, is said to have requested that it be carried in the woman's belly at the time it first met her and to have entered her body through her sexual part. Thus associated with women, the *hu* or *evu* is considered both maleficent and beneficent. It is at times equated with devil and sorcery, other times with prophecy and anti-sorcery. S/He who is said to "have a *hu*" is both feared and admired. S/He is the one who sees the invisible, moves with ease in the night-world as if in broad daylight, and is endowed with uncommon, exceptional intelligence, penetration, and intuition.[29] Woman and magic. Her power resides in her belly—Our Mother's belly—for her cure is not an isolated act but a total social phenomenon. Sorcery, according to numerous accounts, is hereditary solely within the matrilineal clan; and a man, in countless cases, can only become a sorcerer (a wizard) through the transmission of power by a sorceress (witch). He who understands the full power of woman and/in storytelling also understands that life is not to be found in the mind nor in the heart, but there where she carries it:

I will tell you something about stories, [he said]
They aren't just entertainment.
Don't be fooled.
They are all we have, you see,
all we have to fight off
illness and death.

You don't have anything
if you don't have the stories. . . .

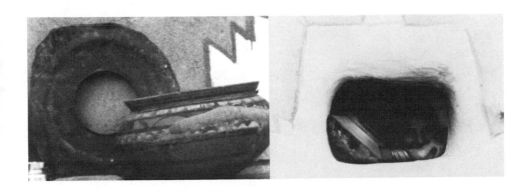

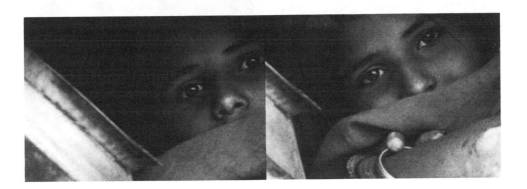

The story is older than my body, my mother's, my grandmother's. For years we have been passing it on so that it may live, shift, and circulate. So that it may become larger than its proper measure, always larger than its own in-significance (Stills from **I-C**)

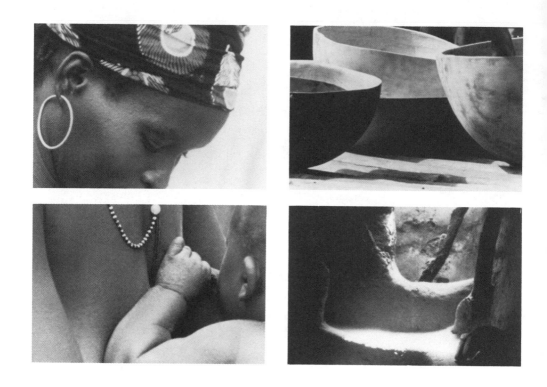

"Speech . . . creates a bond of coming-and-going which generates movement and rhythm . . . life and action" (A. Hampate Ba) (Stills from **NS**)

(Stills from **SVGNN**)

He rubbed his belly.
I keep them here [he said]
Here, put your hand on it
See, it is moving
There is life here
for the people.[30]

The story as a cure and a protection is at once musical, historical, poetical, ethical, educational, magical, and religious. In many parts of the world, the healers are known as the living memories of the people. Not only do they hold esoteric and technical knowledge, but they are also kept closely informed of the problems of their communities and are entrusted with all family affairs. In other words, they know everyone's story. Concerned with the slightest incident, they remain very alert to their entourage and heedful of their patients' talks. They derive their power from *listening* to the others and *absorbing* daily realities. While they cure, they take into them their patients' possessions and obsessions and let the latter's illnesses become theirs. Their actions imply a personal investment of which the healing technics form only a part and are a reflection. "I see the patient's psychic life," many of them say, "nothing is hidden from me." Dis-ease breeds dis-ease; life engenders life. The very close relationship these healers maintain with their patients remains the determining factor of the cure. Curing means re-generating, for understanding is creating. The principle of healing rests on *reconciliation*, hence the necessity for the family and/or the community to cooperate, partake in, and witness the recovery, de-possession, regeneration of the sick. The act of healing is therefore a socio-cultural act, a collective, motherly undertaking. (Here, it is revealing to remember that male healers often claim to be wedded to at least two wives: a terrestrial one *and* a spiritual one. The spiritual wife or the "woman spirit" protects the healer and is the source of his powers. She is the one who "has knowledge" and from whom he seeks advice in all matters. When she becomes too demanding and too possessive, it is said that only one person can send her away: the healer's own mother.)[31] The storyteller, besides being a great mother, a teacher, a poetess, a warrior, a musician, a historian, a fairy, and a witch, is a healer and a protectress. Her chanting or telling of stories, as Marmon Silko notices, has the power of bringing us together, especially when there is sickness, fear, and grief. " 'When they look / they see only objects,' / They fear / they never stop fearing / but they see not fear the living thing. / They follow not its movements / for they fear not to fear. / 'They destroy what they fear. / They fear themselves.' / They destroy the stories / let these be confused or forgotten / let these be only stories / They would like that . . . "

Stolen rivers and mountains
the stolen land will eat their hearts
and jerk their mouths from the Mother.
The people will starve.[32]

"Tell it the way they tell it"

It is a commonplace for those who consider the story to be just a story to believe that, in order to appropriate the "traditional" storytellers' powers and to produce the same effects as theirs, it suffices to "look for the structure of their narratives." *See them as they see each other*, so goes the (anthropological) creed. "Tell it the way *they* tell it instead of imposing *our* structure," they repeat with the best of intentions and a conscience so clear that they pride themselves on it. Disease breeds disease. Those who function best within definite structures and spend their time structuring their own or their peers' existences must obviously "look for" that which, according to their "findings" and analyses, is supposed to be "the structure of their [the storytellers'] narratives." What we "look for" is un/fortunately what we shall find. The anthropologist, as we already know, does not *find* things; s/he *makes* them. And makes them up. The structure is therefore not something given, entirely external to the person who structures, but a projection of that person's way of handling realities, here narratives. It is perhaps difficult for an analytical or analytically trained mind to admit that recording, gathering, sorting, deciphering, analyzing and synthesizing, dissecting and articulating are already "imposing our [/a] structure," a structural activity, a structuring of the mind, a whole mentality. (Can one "look for a structure" without structuring?) But it is particularly difficult for a dualistic or dualistically trained mind to recognize that "looking for the structure of their narratives" already involves the separation of the structure from the narratives, of the structure from that which is structured, of the narrative from the narrated, and so on. It is, once more, as if form and content stand apart; as if the structure can remain fixed, immutable, independent of and unaffected by the changes the narratives undergo; as if a structure can only function as a standard mold within the old determinist schema of cause and product. Listen, for example, to what a man of the West had to say on the form of the story:

> Independent of the content which the story carries, and which may vary from history to nonsense, is the form of the story which is practically the same in all stories. The content is varied and particular, the form is the same and universal. Now there are four main elements in the form of each story, viz. the beginning, the development, the climax, and the end.[33]

Just like the Western drama with its four or five acts. A drama whose naïve claim to universality would not fail to make this man of the West our laughingstock. "A good story," another man of the West asserted, "must have a beginning that rouses interest, a succession of events that is orderly and complete, a climax that forms the story's point, and an end that leaves the mind at rest."[34] No criteria other than those quoted here show a more thorough investment of the Western mind. *Get them*—children, story-believers—*at the start; make your point* by ordering events to a definite *climax;* then *round out to completion;* descend to a rapid close—not one, for example, that puzzles or keeps them puzzling over the story, but one that *leaves the mind at rest.* In other words, to be "good" a story must be built in conformity with the ready-made idea some people—Western adults—have of reality, that is to say, a set of prefabricated schemata (prefabricated by whom?) they value out of habit, conservatism, and ignorance (of other ways of telling and listening to stories). If these criteria are to be adopted, then countless non-Western stories will fall straight into the category of "bad" stories. Unless one makes it up or invents a reason for its absence, one of these four elements required always seems to be missing. The stories in question either have no development, no climax that forms the story's point, or no end that leaves the mind at rest. (One can say of the majority of these stories that their endings precisely refute such generalization and rationale for they offer no security of this kind. An example among endless others is the moving story of "The Laguna People" passed on by Marmon Silko, which ends with a little girl, her sister, and the people turning into stone while they sat on top of a mesa, after they had escaped the flood in their home village below. Because of the disquieting nature of the resolution here, the storytellers [Marmon Silko and her aunt] then add, as a compromise to the fact-oriented mind of today's audience: "The story ends there. / Some of the stories / Aunt Susi told / have this kind of ending. / There are no explanations."[35] There is no point [to be] made either.) "Looking for the structure of *their* narratives" so as to "tell it the way *they* tell it" is an attempt at remedying this ignorance of other ways of telling and listening (and, obviously, at re-validating the nativist discourse). In doing so, however, rare are those who realize that what they come up with is not "structure of *their* narratives" but a reconstruction of the story that, at best, makes a number of its functions appear. Rare are those who acknowledge the unavoidable transfer of values in the "search" and admit that "the attempt will remain largely illusory: we shall never know if the other, into whom we cannot, after all, dissolve, fashions from the elements of [her/]his social existence a synthesis exactly superimposable on that which we have worked out."[36] The attempt will remain illusory as long as the controlled succession of certain mental operations which constitutes the structural activity is not made explicit and dealt with—not just mentioned. Life is not a (Western) drama of four or five acts. Sometimes it just drifts along; it may go on year after year without development, without climax, without definite beginnings or endings. Or it may accumulate climax upon climax, and if one chooses to mark it with beginnings and endings, then everything has a beginning and an ending. There are, in this sense, no good or bad stories. In life, we usually don't know when an event is occurring; we think it is starting when it is already ending; and we don't see its in/significance. The present, which saturates the total field of our environment, is often invisible to us. The structural activity that does not carry on the cleavage between form and content but emphasizes the interrelation of the material and the intelligible is an activity in which structure should remain an unending question: one that speaks him/her as s/he speaks it, brings it to intelligibility.

"The story must be told. There must not be any lies"

"Looking for the structure of their narratives" is like looking for the pear shape in Erik Satie's musical composition *Trois Pièces en Forme de Poire* (Three Pieces in a Pear Shape). (The composition was written after Satie met with Claude Debussy, who criticized his music for "lacking of form.") If structure, as a man (R. Barthes) pertinently defines it, is "the residual deposit of duration," then again, rare are those who can handle it by letting it come, instead of hunting for it or hunting it down, filling it with their own marks and markings so as to consign it to the meaningful and lay claim to it. *"They see no life / When they look / they see only objects."* The ready-made idea they have of reality prevents their perceiving the story as a living thing, an organic process, a way of life. What is taken for stories, only stories, are fragments of/in life, fragments that never stop interacting while being complete in themselves. A story in Africa may last three months. The storyteller relates it night after night, continually, or s/he starts it one night and takes it up again from that point three months later. Meanwhile, as the occasion arises, s/he may start on yet another story. Such is life . . . :

> The gussucks [the Whites] did not understand the story; they could not see the way it must be told, year after year as the old man had done, without lapse or silence. . . .
> "It began a long time ago," she intoned steadily . . . she did not pause or hesitate; she went on with the story, and she never stopped. . . .[37]

"Storyteller," from which these lines are excerpted, is another story, another gift of life passed on by Marmon Silko. It presents an example of multiple storytelling in which story and life merge, the story being as complex as life and life being as simple as a story. The story of "Storyteller" is the layered making of four storytellers: Marmon Silko, the woman in the story, her grandmother, and the person referred to as "the old man." Except for Marmon Silko who plays here the role of the coordinator, each of these three storytellers has her/his own story to live and live with. Despite the differences in characters or in subject matter, their stories closely interact and constantly overlap. The woman makes of her story a continuation of her grandmother's, which was left with no ending—the grandmother being thereby compelled to bear it (the story) until her death, her knees and knuckles swollen grotesquely, "swollen with anger" as she explained it. She bore it, knowing that her granddaughter will have to bear it too: "It will take a long time," she said, "but the story must be told. There must not be any lies." Sometime after her death, exactly when does not matter, when the time comes, the granddaughter picks up the story where her grandmother left it and carries it to its end accordingly, the way "it must be told." She carries it to a certain completion by bringing in death where she intends to have it in her story: the white storeman who lied in her grandma's story and was the author of her parents' death would have to pay for his lies, but his death would also have to be of his own making. The listener/reader does not (have to) know whether the storeman in the granddaughter's story is the same as the one who, according to the grand-mother, "left right after that [after he lied and killed]" (hence making it apparently impossible for the old woman to finish her story). A storeman becomes *the* storeman, the man in the store, the man in the story. (The truthfulness of the story, as we already know, does not limit itself to the realm of facts.) Which story? *The* story. What grandma began, granddaughter completes and passes on to be further completed. As a storyteller, the woman (the granddaughter) does not directly kill; she decides when and where that storeman will find death, but she does not carry out a hand-to-hand fight and her murder of him is no murder in the common, factual sense of the term: all she needs to do is set in motion the necessary forces and let them act on their own.

> They asked her again, what happened to the man from the Northern Com-mercial Store. "He lied to them. He told them it was safe to drink. But I will not lie. . . . I killed him," she said, "but I don't lie."

When she is in jail, the Gussuck attorney advises her to tell the court the *truth*, which is that it was an accident, that the storeman ran after her in the cold and fell through the ice. That's all what she has to say—then "they will let [her] go home. Back to [her] village."

"I intended that he die. The story must be told as it is"
(Stills from **NS**)

"Civilization is not mere advance in technology and in the material aspects of life. We should remember it is an abstract noun and indicates a state of living and not things" (C. Rajagopalachari) (Stills from **I-C**)

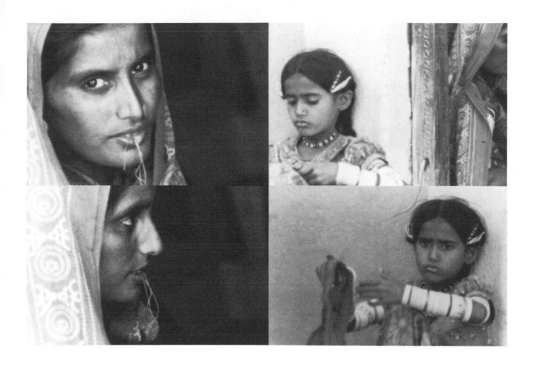

Storytelling: her words set into motion the forces that lie dormant in things and beings (Stills from **I-C**)

> She shook her head. "I will not change the story, not even to escape this place and go home. I intended that he die. The story must be told as it is." The attorney exhaled loudly; his eyes looked tired. "Tell her that she could not have killed him that way. He was a white man. He ran after her without a parka or mittens. She could not have planned that."[38]

When the helpful, conscientious (full-of-the-white-man's-complex-of-superiority) attorney concludes that he will do "all [he] can for her" and will explain to the judge that "her mind is confused," she laughs out loud and finally decides to tell him the story anew: "*It began a long time ago . . .*" (my italics). He says she could not have killed that white man because, again, for him the story is just a story. But Thought-Woman, Spider-Woman is a fairy and a witch who protects her people and tells stories to effect cures. As she names Death, Death appears. The spell is cast. Only death gives an ending to the stories in "Storyteller." (The old man's story of the giant bear overlaps with the granddaughter's story and ends the moment the old man—the storyteller—dies.) Marmon Silko as a storyteller never loses sight of the difference between truth and fact. Her naming retains the accuracy and magic of our grand mothers' storytelling without ever confining itself to the realm of factual naming. It is accurate because it is at once extremely flexible and rigid, not because it wishes to stick to certain rules of correctness for reasons of mere conservatism (scholars studying traditional storytelling are often impressed by the storyteller's "necessity of telling the stories correctly," as they put it). It is accurate because it partakes in the setting into motion of forces that lie dormant in us. Because, as African storytellers sing, "the tongue that falsifies the word / taints the blood of [her/]him that lies."[39] Because she who bears it in her belly cannot cut herself off from herself. Off from the bond of coming-and-going. Off from her great mothers.

"May my story be beautiful and unwind like a long thread . . . , she recites as she begins her story. Here she chants the time-honored formula that opens the tales of Kabyle folksingers, but what she chants, in a way, is a variant of what her African griotte-sisters chant every time they set about composing on life: tell me so that I can tell my hearers what I have heard from you who heard it from your mother and your great mother. . . . Each woman, like each people, has her own way of unrolling the ties that bind. Storytelling, the oldest form of building historical consciousness in community, constitutes a rich oral legacy, whose values have regained all importance recently, especially in the context of writings by women of color. She who works at un-learning the dominant language of "civilized" missionaries also has to learn how to un-write and write anew. And she often does so by re-establishing the contact with her foremothers, so that living tradition can never congeal into fixed forms, so that life keeps on nurturing life, so that what is understood as the Past continues to provide the link for the Present and the Future. As our elder Lao Tzu says, "Without allowance for filling, a valley will run dry; / Without allowance for growing, creation will stop functioning." Tradition as on-going commitment, and in women's own terms. The story is beautiful, because or therefore it unwinds like a thread. A long thread, for there is no end in sight. Or the end she reaches leads actually to another end, another opening, another "residual deposit of duration." Every woman partakes in the chain of guardianship and of transmission—in other words, of creation. Every griotte who dies is a whole library that burns down. Tell it so that they can tell it. So that it may become larger than its measure, always larger than its own in/significance. In this horizontal and vertical vertigo, she carries the story on, motivated at once by the desire to finish it and the necessity to remind herself and others that "it's never finished." A lifetime story. More than a lifetime. One that will be picked up where it is left; when, it does not matter. For the time is already set. "It will take a long time . . .," the grandmother ends; "it began long ago . . .," the granddaughter starts. The time is set, she said; not in terms of when exactly but of what: what exactly must be told, and how. "There must not be any lies." Like Maxine Hong Kingston who decided to tell the world the forbidden story of her tabooed aunt, the "No Name Woman," Marmon Silko's granddaughter-storyteller, opens the spell cast upon her people, by re-setting into motion what was temporarily delayed in the story of her grandmother. The burden of the story-truth. She knew that during her own lifetime the moment would come when she would be able to assume her responsibility and resume the grandmother's interrupted story-trajectory. She killed the one who lied to her people, who actively participated in the slow extinction of her race. She killed Him. She killed the white storeman in "her story" which is not "just a story": "I intended that he die. The story must be told as it is." To ask, like the white attorney, whether the story she tells makes any sense, whether it is factually possible, whether it is true or not is to cause confusion by an incorrect question. Difference here is not understood as difference. Her (story) world remains therefore irreducibly foreign to Him. The man can't hear it the way she means it. He sees her as victim, as unfortunate object of hazard. "Her mind is confused," he concludes. She views herself as the teller, the un-making subject, the agent of the storeman's death, the moving force of the story. She didn't know when exactly she would be able to act in concordance with fate (she is also fate), but she planned and waited for the ripe moment to come, so that what appeared as an accident was carefully matured. Her sense of the story overflows the boundaries of patriarchal time and truth. It overflows the notion of story as finished product ("just a story")—one neatly wrapped, that rounds off with a normative finale and "leaves the mind at rest." Marmon Silko's "Storyteller" keeps the reader puzzling over the story as it draws to a close. Again, truth does not make sense. It exceeds measure: the woman storyteller sees her vouching for it as a defiance of a whole system of the white man's lies. She values this task, this responsibility over immediate release (her being freed from imprisonment through the attorney's advice), over immediate enlightenment and gratification (vengeance for the sake of vengeance). Even if the telling condemns her present life, what is more important is to (re-)tell the story as she thinks it should be told; in other words, to maintain the difference that allows (her) truth to live on. The difference. He does not hear or see. He cannot give. Never the given, for there is no end in sight.

There are these stories that just have to be told in the same way the wind goes blowing across the mesa
   —Leslie Marmon Silko, "Stories and Their Tellers"

A BEDTIME STORY

Once upon a time,
an old Japanese legend
goes as told
by Papa,
an old woman traveled through
many small villages
seeking refuge
for the night.
Each door opened
a sliver
in answer to her knock
then closed.
Unable to walk
any further
she wearily climbed a hill
found a clearing
and there lay down to rest
a few moments to catch
her breath.

The villagetown below
lay asleep except
for a few starlike lights.

Suddenly the clouds opened
and a full moon came into view
over the town.

The old woman sat up
turned toward
the village town
and in supplication
called out
Thank you people
of the village,
if it had not been for your
kindness
in refusing me a bed
for the night
these humble eyes would never
have seen this
memorable sight.

Papa paused, I waited.
In the comfort of our
hilltop home in Seattle
overlooking the valley,
I shouted
"That's the END?"

—Mitsuye Yamada, *Camp Notes*

Notes

I. Commitment from the Mirror-Writing Box

1. Virginia Woolf, *Women and Writing* (New York: Harcourt Brace Jovanovich, 1979), p. 54.
2. Tillie Olsen, *Silences* (1978, rpt. New York: Delta/Seymour Lawrence Ed., 1980), pp. 13, 39.
3. Denise Paulme, ed., *Women of Tropical Africa*, tr. H. M. Wright (1963, rpt. Berkeley: Univ. of California Press, 1974), p. 2.
4. hattie gossett, "Who Told You Anybody Wants To Hear From You? You Ain't Nothing But a Black Woman!" *This Bridge Called My Back: Writings by Radical Women of Color*, ed. Cherríe Morraga & Gloria Anzaldúa (Watertown, Mass.: Persephone Press, 1981), p. 175.
5. Gloria Anzaldúa, "Speaking in Tongues: A Letter to 3rd World Women Writers," *This Bridge*, p. 166.
6. Sylvia Plath, *The Bell Jar* (1971, rpt. New York: Bantam Books, 1981), see Biographical Note by Lois Ames, p. 211.
7. Emma Santos, *L'Itinéraire psychiatrique* (Paris: Des Femmes, 1977), pp. 46–47. For previous quotes see pp. 47, 50, 125 (my translations).
8. Toni Cade Bambara, "What It Is I Think I'm Doing Anyhow," *The Writer on Her Work*, ed. J. Sternburg (New York: W. W. Norton, 1980), p. 167.
9. "Commitment: Toni Cade Bambara Speaks," interview with Beverly Guy-Sheftall in *Sturdy Black Bridges: Visions of Black Women in Literature*, ed. R. P. Bell, B. J. Parker, & B. Guy-Sheftall (New York: Anchor/Doubleday, 1979), p. 232.
10. Ezekiel Mphahlele, *Voices in the Whirlwind* (New York: Hill & Wang, 1972), pp. 186–87.
11. Ibid., p. 196.
12. Franz Fanon, *Black Skin White Masks*, tr. Charles Lam Markmann (New York: Grove Press, 1967), p. 8.
13. Jean-Paul Sartre, *Situations, II. Qu'est-ce que la littérature?* (Paris: Gallimard, 1948), pp. 112, 97.
14. Margaret Walker, "On Being Female, Black, and Free," *The Writer and Her Work*, pp. 95, 102, 106.
15. Jacques Rabemananjara, "Le Poète noir et son peuple," *Présence Africaine*, no. 16 (Oct.–Nov. 1957), pp. 10–13.
16. Aimé Césaire, *Return to My Native Land* (Paris: Présence Africaine, 1971), pp. 60–62.
17. Nikki Giovanni, *Gemini: An Extended Autobiographical Statement on My First Twenty-Five Years of Being a Black Poet* (New York: Viking Press, 1971), pp. 95–96.
18. Alice Walker, "Saving The Life That Is Your Own: The Importance of Models in The Artist's Life," *The Third Woman: Minority Women Writers of The United States*, ed. D. Fisher (Boston: Houghton Mifflin, 1980), p. 158.
19. Wole Soyinka, *Myth, Literature, and the African World* (New York: Cambridge Univ. Press, 1976), p. 138.
20. Mphahlele, *Voices in the Whirlwind*, p. 189.

21. Michel Beaujour, "Flight out of Time," *Literature and Revolution,* ed. J. Ehrmann (Boston: Beacon Press, 1967), p. 32.

22. Cade Bambara, "Commitment . . .," *Sturdy Black Bridges,* p. 236.

23. Joan Didion, "Why I Write," *The Writer on Her Work,* p. 20.

24. Roland Barthes, *The Pleasure of the Text,* tr. R. Miller (New York: Hill & Wang, 1975), p. 51.

25. Roland Barthes, *Writing Degree Zero,* tr. A. Lavers & C. Smith (New York: Hill & Wang, 1967), p. 63.

26. *Woman as Writer,* ed. J. L. Webber and J. Grumman (Boston: Houghton Mifflin, 1978), p. 85.

27. Ibid., pp. 15–16.

28. Ibid., p. 98 ("The Nature and Aim of Fiction").

29. Ibid., p. 37.

30. Virginia Woolf, *A Room of One's Own* (New York: Harcourt Brace Jovanovich, 1929), pp. 79–80.

31. Barthes, *Writing Degree Zero,* p. 15.

32. Susan Griffin, "Thoughts on Writing: A Diary," *The Writer on Her Work,* p. 110.

33. Both the images of the Japanese boxes and the Taoist empty mirrors as related to writing have been discussed in Trinh T. Minh-ha, "The Plural Void: Barthes and Asia," *Sub-Stance* 36, vol. XI, no. 3 (1982), pp. 41–50.

34. *Woman as Writer,* p. 16 ("Journal").

35. Margaret Atwood, "Paradoxes and Dilemmas, The Woman as Writer," *Woman as Writer,* p. 182.

36. Dilys Laing, "The Double Goer," *By a Woman Writt,* ed. J. Goulianos (1973, rpt. Baltimore: Penguin Books, 1974), pp. 325–26.

37. Hélène Cixous, *Vivre l'orange* (Paris: Des Femmes, 1979), pp. 36,38, 40.

38. Didion, "Why I Write," *The Writer on Her Work,* p. 21.

39. Cixous, *Vivre l'orange,* p. 46.

40. Diana Chang, "Woolgathering, Ventriloquism, and the Double Life," *The Third Woman,* pp. 457–58.

41. Quoted by Karen Gould in "Setting Words Free: Feminist Writing in Quebec," *Signs* 6, no. 4 (Summer 1981), p. 629.

42. Hélène Cixous, "The Laugh of the Medusa," tr. K. Cohen and P. Cohen, *Signs* 1, no. 4 (Summer 1976), pp. 880, 886.

43. Anaïs Nin, "Diary," *By A Woman Writt,* pp. 294, 299.

44. Annie Leclerc, *Paroles de femme* (Paris: Grasset, 1974), pp. 11–12 (my translation).

45. For a detailed analysis of these images, see Irma Garcia, *Promenade femmilière,* vol. 2 (Paris: Des Femmes, 1981).

46. I have discussed the relationship between body, mother, cry (voice), hand, and life in Trinh T. Minh-ha, "L'innécriture: Féminisme et littérature," *French Forum* 8, no. 1 (January 1983), pp. 45–63.

47. Cixous, "The Laugh of the Medusa," p. 884.

48. Janice Raymond, "The Illusion of Androgyny," *Quest* 2, no. 1 (Summer 1975), p. 66.

49. Maurice Blanchot, *The Writing of the Disaster,* tr. A. Smock (Lincoln: Univ. of Nebraska Press, 1986), p. 38.

50. Marguerite Duras, "Smothered Creativity," *New French Feminism,* ed. E. Marks & I. de Courtivon (Amherst: Univ. of Massachusetts Press, 1980), p. 111.

51. Catherine Clément. *Les Fils de Freud sont fatigués* (Paris: Grasset, 1978), p. 137 (my translation).

52. Duras, in *New French Feminism,* pp. 174–75.

53. Blanchot, *The Writing of the Disaster,* p. 38.

54. Hélène Cixous & Catherine Clément, *The Newly Born Woman*, tr. Betsy Wing (Minneapolis: Univ. of Minnesota Press, 1986), pp. 146, 92.

55. Monique Wittig & Sande Zeig, *Lesbian Peoples. Material for a Dictionary* (New York: Avon, 1979), p. 166.

56. Gayatri Chakravorty Spivak, Interview, *Art Network* 16 (Winter 1985), p. 26.

57. Cixous, "Castration or Decapitation?" *Signs* 7, 1 (Autumn 1981), p. 51.

II. The Language of Nativism

1. Roland Barthes, *A Lover's Discourse*, tr. R. Howard (New York: Hill & Wang, 1978), p. 135.

2. Quoted in Marcel Griaule, *Conversations with Ogotemmêli* (1965, rpt. New York: Oxford Univ. Press, 1975), p. 82.

3. Roland Barthes, *Critical Essays*, tr. R. Howard (Evanston, Ill.: Northwestern Univ. Press, 1972), p. xvii.

4. Ivan Illich, "Vernacular Values," *CoEvolution Quarterly* 22 (1980), p. 27. See also Claude Lévi-Strauss, *Race et histoire* (Paris: Gonthier, 1961), pp. 19–21.

5. Lévi-Strauss, *Race*, p. 22 (my translation).

6. Vine Deloria, Jr., *Custer Died for Your Sins* (New York: Avon Books, 1969), pp. 189–90.

7. Jean Piaget quoted by G. Berthoud. See Berthoud's reply to Diane Lewis's essay "Anthropology and Colonialism," *Current Anthropology* 14, no. 5 (1973), p. 592.

8. Bronislaw Malinowski, *Argonauts of the Western Pacific* (1922, rpt. New York: E. P. Dutton, 1961), p. 8.

9. Ibid., pp. 9–10.

10. Quoted in *The Ethnography of Malinowski*, ed. M. W. Young (Boston: Routledge & Kegan Paul, 1979), p. 9.

11. Malinowski, *Argonauts*, p. 12.

12. Ibid., p. 24.

13. Ibid., pp. 12, 11 (original italics).

14. Raymond Firth, "The Sceptical Anthropologist? Social Anthropology and Marxist View on Society" (Inaugural Radcliffe-Brown Lecture in Social Anthropology), *Proceedings of the British Academy* 58 (1972), pp. 26–27.

15. Stanislas S. Adotevi, *Négritude et négrologues* (Paris: UGE, 1972), p. 176 (my translation).

16. Malinowski, *Argonauts*, p. 25.

17. Stanley Diamond, "Anthropology in Question," *Reinventing Anthropology*, ed. D. Hymes (New York: Random House, 1972), pp. 401–3.

18. The three quotes are from several anthropologists' responses to Diane Lewis's essay, pp. 592–93.

19. Claude Lévi-Strauss, *The Scope of Anthropology*, tr. S. Ortner Paul & R. A. Paul (1967, rpt. London: Jonathan Cape, 1971), p. 14.

20. Claude Lévi-Strauss, *The Raw and the Cooked*, tr. John and Doreen Weightman (New York: Harper & Row, 1969), pp. 1–14.

21. Lévi-Strauss, *Scope*, p. 15.

22. Malinowski, *Argonauts*, pp. 327, 326.

23. Lévi-Strauss, *Scope*, p. 26.

24. Lévi-Strauss, *The Raw and the Cooked*, p. 5.

25. Ibid, pp. 18, 12.

26. Barthes, *Critical Essays*, p. 160. I have discussed the concept of writing/package more extensively in Trinh T. Minh-ha, "The Plural Void: Barthes and Asia," *Sub-Stance* 36, vol. XI, no.3 (1982), pp. 41–50.

27. Lévi-Strauss, *The Raw and the Cooked*, p. 12.

28. Lévi-Strauss, *Scope*, p. 26.

29. Claude Lévi-Strauss, *The Savage Mind* (Chicago: Univ. of Chicago Press, 1966), p. 19. *Bricoleur* is a French word whose closest equivalent in English would be "tinker" or "Jack of all trades." It is used by Lévi-Strauss in opposition to the scientist, be he an engineer, a physicist, or a chemist.

30. Ibid., p. 17.

31. Jacques Derrida, *Writing and Difference*, tr. Alan Bass (Chicago: Univ. of Chicago Press, 1978), p. 285.

32. Lévi-Strauss, *The Raw and the Cooked*, p. 7; compare with the concept of "total" in *The Scope of Anthropology*.

33. Lévi-Strauss, *The Savage Mind*, pp. 20, 22.

34. Georges Charbonnier, *Entretiens avec Lévi-Strauss* (Paris: UGE, 1961), p. 182.

35. Lévi-Strauss, *Scope*, p. 20.

36. Ibid., pp. 42–46.

37. Peter Farb, *Man's Rise to Civilization* (New York: Bantam Books, Inc., 1978), p. 16.

38. Clifford Geertz, *The Interpretation of Culture* (New York: Basic Books, 1973), p. 30.

39. Lévi-Strauss in *Entretiens*, pp. 19, 57.

40. Lévi-Strauss, *Scope*, p. 14.

41. Jacob Bronowski, *The Ascent of Man* (Boston: Little, Brown, 1973), p. 24, quoted by C. Miller & K. Swift in *Words and Women* (New York: Anchor/Doubleday, 1977), p. 18.

42. James D. McCawley, "Letter to the Editor," *New York Times Magazine*, 10 Nov. 1974, quoted in *Words and Women*, p. 29.

43. Maxine Hong Kingston, "The Coming Book," *The Writer on Her Work*, ed. J. Sternburg (New York: W. W. Norton, 1980), p. 84.

44. Barthes, *Lover's Discourse*, p. 185.

45. The distinction between *gossip* and *conversation* has been made by R. Barthes, *Lover's Discourse*, p. 183. Aristotle's use of the word *anthropology* to mean *gossip* has been mentioned by Ivan Illich, *Gender* (New York: Pantheon Books, 1982), p. 132.

46. Adotevi, pp. 182, 197 (my translation).

47. Barthes, *Lover's Discourse*, p. 184.

48. Bronislaw Malinowski, *The Sexual Life of Savages* (New York: Harcourt Brace Jovanovich, 1929). All quotes from this book are on pp. 281–87, 330–34.

49. Geertz, p. 12.

50. Barthes, *Pleasure*, pp. 27–28.

51. Geertz, p. 15.

52. Malinowski, *Argonauts*, p. 23.

53. Geertz, p. 29.

54. Ibid., p. 13–14.

55. Malinowski, *Argonauts*, p. 25.

56. Adotevi, p. 182 (my translation).

57. Malinowski, *Argonauts*, p. 22 (my italics); p. 11.

58. Ibid., pp. 23, 454.

59. Barthes, *Pleasure*, p. 40.

60. Malinowski, *The Dynamics of Culture Change*, ed. P. M. Kaberry (New Haven, Conn.: Yale Univ. Press, 1945), pp. 3–4.

61. B. Baldwin, "Traditional and Cultural Aspects of Trobriand Island Chiefs," unpubl. ms., pp. 17–18; and J. Kasaipwalova, " 'Modernizing' Melanesian Society—Why and For Whom?" *Priorities in Melanesian Development*, ed. R. J. May (Sixth Waigani Seminar, Australian National Univ, and Univ. of Papua New Guinea), p. 454. Both are quoted in Young, *The Ethnography of Malinowski*, pp. 15, 17.

62. Malinowski, *A Diary in the Strict Sense of the Term* (New York: Harcourt, Brace & World, 1967). See especially pp. 261, 276. The two quotes that follow are on pp. 167, 264.

63. Lévi-Strauss, *Scope*, p. 14.

64. Cultural anthropology has, more recently, attempted to address some of the questions raised in this chapter. Of interest here, for example, are the works of writers of *Writing Culture: The Poetics and Politics of Ethnography* (Berkeley: Univ. of California Press, 1986), particularly those of James Clifford, who has consistently exposed the workings of ethnographic authority and ideology in his analyses. It is, however, worth mentioning that Georges Marcus, who co-edited *Writing Culture* with Clifford, closes the book by stating: "The task of the Santa Fe seminar from which these essays emerged was to introduce a *literary* consciousness to ethnographic practice by showing various ways in which ethnographies can be read and written. . . . The question for the anthropologist is, then, how consequential this *literary therapy* should be—does it *merely* add a new critical *appreciation* of ethnography . . . or does it clear the way for reconceptualizing anthropological *careers* and *valorizing* innovations in strategies for projects that link fieldwork and writing?" (my italics). Besides its more obvious reassuring tone (reassuring to anthropological careers), such a closing statement makes it quite easy for anthropologists to bypass, if not dismiss, the issues raised by confining them to the realm of "literature" ("these are preoccupations that originally spring from people with a literary background—not a scientific one"). Not only is this literary consciousness viewed merely as "a new critical appreciation of ethnography" or as a preceding step to the reconceptualization and revalorizing of anthropological careers (as I have mentioned earlier, opening up "a self/other-referential language-space where the observing-writing subject watches himself observe and write while foregrounding the specific instances of discourse involved in his own writing" has little in common with the moralistic self-knowledge and self-criticism aiming at "improvement"), but "literary" in Marcus's context does not constitute a site of discussion nor is the word problematized in its contemporary, controversial connotations. What Clifford starts out drawing attention to in the introduction— namely, the notion of interdisciplinary work as "a new object that belongs to no one" (Barthes) and of literature as a transient category—needs to be taken fully into account if a radical critique of anthropological writing is to be carried out. To understand the necessity of an ongoing critique of the West's most confident prevailing discourses is to understand, as Julia Kristeva demonstrates, that "because it focuses on the *process* of meaning within language and ideology—from 'ego' to history—literary practice remains the missing link in the sociocommunicative or subjective-transcendental fabric of the so-called human sciences" (*Desire in Language*, p. 98, her italics). This would make hardly surprising the current work effected, for example, on the "science of the subject" in literary practice as well as on the "ethnographies fictions" in textual theory. Certainly the essays of *Writing Culture* set into relief the representational practices that generate and sustain ethnographic discourse. They successfully point to the textual operations that contribute to create an aura of legitimacy surrounding the production of knowledge and to direct the reader's attention away from their modes of address as well as their search for unmediated meaning in the event observed. But again, as cultural writing itself, can a critique of ethnographic writing be done without reflecting on its own writing? Without, through its practice of language, "unsettling the identity of meaning and speaking/writing subject"?

III. Difference

Our special thanks goes to Mitsuye Yamada for the authorization to quote her poems in this book.

1. Audre Lorde, "The Master's Tools Will Never Dismantle the Master's House," *This Bridge Called My Back: Writings by Radical Women of Color*, ed. C. Morraga & G. Anzaldúa (Watertown, Mass.: Persephone Press, 1981), p. 99.

2. Charles A. W. Manning. "In Defense of Apartheid," *Africa Yesterday and Today*, ed. C. D. Moore & A. Dunbar (New York: Bantam, 1968), p. 287.

3. Ibid., p. 289.

4. Jan Christiaan Smuts, quoted in Louis Fischer, *Gandhi: His Life and Message for the World* (New York: New American Library, 1954), p. 25.

5. General Louis Botha, quoted in ibid.

6. Manning, p. 287.

7. Gayatri Chakravorty Spivak, "The Politics of Interpretations," *Critical Inquiry* 9, no. 1 (1982), p. 278.

8. Gloria Anzaldúa, "Speaking in Tongues: A Letter to 3rd World Women Writers," *This Bridge*, pp. 167–68.

9. Mitsuye Yamada, "Asian Pacific American Women and Feminism," *This Bridge*, p. 71.

10. Lorde, "The Master's Tools . . .," p. 100.

11. Alice Walker, "One Child of One's Own: A Meaningful Digression Within the Work(s)," *The Writer on Her Work*, ed. J. Sternburg (New York: W. W. Norton, 1980), p. 137.

12. Leslie Marmon Silko, "Lullaby," *The Ethnic American Woman*, ed. E. Blicksilver (Dubuque, Iowa: Kendall/Hunt, 1978), p. 57.

13. Virginia Woolf, *A Room of One's Own* (New York: Harcourt Brace Jovanovich, 1929), p. 48.

14. "The Master's Tools . . .," p. 100.

15. Ellen Pence, "Racism—A White Issue," *But Some of Us Are Brave*, ed. G. T. Hull, P. B. Scott, & B. Smith (Old Westbury, N.Y.: Feminist Press, 1982), p. 46.

16. Ibid., pp. 46–47.

17. Barbara Smith, "Racism and Women's Studies," *But Some of Us Are Brave*, p. 49.

18. Mitsuye Yamada, "Invisibility Is An Unnatural Disaster: Reflections of an Asian American Woman," *This Bridge*, pp. 36–37.

19. Adrienne Rich, *On Lies, Secrets and Silence* (New York: W. W. Norton, 1979), pp. 38–39.

20. Joanne Harumi Sechi, "Being Japanese-American Doesn't Mean 'Made in Japan,' " *The Third Woman. Minority Women Writers of the United States*, ed. D. Fisher (Boston: Houghton Mifflin Cie., 1980), p. 444.

21. "Asian Pacific . . .," pp. 74–75.

22. I have discussed at length the notions of non-dualistic thinking and of multiple presence in Trinh T. Minh-ha, *Un Art sans oeuvre. L'Anonymat dans les arts contemporains* (Troy, Mich.: International Books Pubs., 1981).

23. Vine Deloria, Jr., *Custer Died for Your Sins* (New York: Avon Books, 1969), p. 86.

24. Excerpts in *Women Poets of Japan*, ed. Kenneth Rexroth and Ikuko Atsumi (New York: New Directions Books, 1977), p. 123.

25. Quoted in Alan W. Watts, *Nature, Man, and Woman* (1958, rpt. New York: Vintage Books, 1970), p. 121.

26. "On Female Identity and Writing by Women," *Critical Inquiry* 8 (Special Issue on *Writing and Sexual Difference*, ed. E. Abel), no. 2 (1981), pp. 348–49, 354, 353.

27. Simone De Beauvoir, *The Second Sex* (1952, rpt. New York: Bantam, 1970), p. 223.

28. Julia Kristeva, "Woman Can Never Be Defined," trans. Marilyn A. August, *New French Feminism*, ed. E. Marks & I. De Courtivon (Amherst: Univ. of Massachusetts Press, 1980), p. 139.

29. "One Child of One's Own . . .," pp. 133–34.

30. Ibid., p. 136.

31. Quoted in *Sturdy Black Bridges. Visions of Black Women in Literature*, ed. R. P. Bell, B. J. Parker, & B. Guy-Sheftall (Garden City, N.Y.: Anchor/Doubleday, 1979), p. xxv.

32. Sojourner Truth, "Speech of Woman's Suffrage," *The Ethnic American Woman*, p. 335.

33. In *New French Feminism*, pp. 214, 219.

34. In *This Bridge*, pp. 95, 97.

35. "Woman Can Never Be Defined," p. 137.

36. Kristeva in an interview with Xavière Gauthier, "Oscillation between Power and Denial," *New French Feminism*, pp. 166–67.

37. Julia Kristeva, "On the Women of China," tr. E. Conroy Kennedy, *Signs* 1, no. 1 (1975), pp. 79, 81.

38. "Woman Can Never Be Defined," p. 137.

39. Ibid., p. 138.

40. Ivan Illich, *Gender* (New York: Pantheon Books, 1982), pp. 128, 131–32.

41. Ibid., p. 20.

42. "One Child of One's Own . . .," p. 133.

43. *Gender*, p. 178.

44. *La Civilisation de la femme dans la tradition africaine* (Paris: Présence Africaine, 1975), English introduction, p. 15.

45. Ibid., French introduction, p. 13 (my translation).

46. Ibid., p. 68. For Ki-Zerbo & T. Awori, see pp. 22, 31–39.

47. See *Feminist Issues* 3, no. 1 (Spring 1983), an issue devoted to a symposium organized by the Women's Studies Program at UC–Berkeley in response to the lectures Illich gave on his concept of gender in 1982 at the University. Of particular interest here is Barbara Christian's paper on "Alternate Versions of the Gendered Past: African Women Writers vs. Illich," which draws attention to the nostalgic undertones of the concept. Although I agree with the paper and do not view it as being in any way incompatible with what has been discussed in this chapter concerning the question of gender, I would rather emphasize the controversial nature of the concept, its very potential to raise issues and to draw attention to aspects of cultural and sexual description that have until recently been minimized if not ignored in many sociological/anthropological analyses. Difference, as pointed out all along in this chapter, should neither be defined by the dominant sex nor by the dominant culture. As another possibly useful tool to unsettle the notion of difference as division or opposition, gender-differentiated-from-sex should therefore not be simply dismissed or denied but problematized, re-contextualized, and re-appropriated or re-affirmed in women's own terms.

48. Ivan Illich, *Shadow Work* (London: Marion Boyars, 1981), p. 57.

49. *La Civilisation*, p. 15.

50. Ibid., p. 369.

51. Ibid., p. 287.

IV. Grandma's Story

1. Theresa Hak Kyung Cha, *Dictée* (New York: Tanam Press, 1982), p. 133.

2. Maxine Hong Kingston, *The Woman Warrior* (1975, rpt. New York: Vintage Books, 1977), p. 235.

3. Herman Harrell Horne, *Story-telling, Questioning and Studying* (New York: Macmillan, 1917), pp. 23–24.

4. *Dictée*, p. 123.

5. Gayl Jones, *Corregidora* (New York: Random House, 1975), p. 9.

6. Ibid., p. 184.

7. *Dictée*, p. 106.

8. Ibid., p. 130.

9. Horne, p. 34.

10. Katherine Dunlap Cather, *Educating by Story-telling* (New York: World Book Company, 1926), pp. 5–6.

11. Clark W. Hetherington, introduction in ibid., pp. xiii–xiv.

12. Anna Birgitta Rooth, *The Importance of Storytelling: A Study Based on Field Work in Northern Alaska* (Uppsala, Sweden: Almqvist & Wiksell, 1976), p. 88.

13. A. Hampate Ba, "The Living Tradition," *General History of Africa, I. Methodology and African Prehistory*, ed. J. Ki Zerbo (UNESCO, Heineman, Univ. of California Press, 1981), p. 167.

14. Froebel quoted in Horne, p. 29.

15. *Dictée*, p. 150.

16. Quoted in Horne, p. 30.

17. Leslie Marmon Silko, "Aunt Susie," *Storyteller* (New York: Seaver Books, 1981), p. 4.

18. Marcel Griaule, *Conversations with Ogotemmêli* (1965, rpt. New York: Oxford Univ. Press, 1975), pp. 26, 138–39.

19. Ba, "The Living Tradition," pp. 170–71.

20. On the part played by women in religious cults and their powers, see Robert Briffault, *The Mothers* (1927, rpt. New York: Atheneum, 1977), especially the chapter on "The Witch and the Priestess," pp. 269–88.

21. Zora Neale Hurston, *Mules and Men*, excerpts in *I Love Myself*, ed. A. Walker (Old Westbury, N.Y.: Feminist Press, 1979), pp. 85, 93, 89.

22. Leslie Marmon Silko, *Ceremony* (New York: Viking Press, 1977), p. 1.

23. "The Living Tradition," p. 171.

24. *Ceremony*, pp. 132–38, or *Storyteller*, pp. 130–37.

25. Quoted in Cather, p. 22.

26. *Woman Warrior*, pp. 23–24.

27. Ibid., pp. 189, 237, 240, 235.

28. *Ceremony*, back cover page.

29. For more information on the *hu* and its relation to women, see Meinrad P. Hebga, *Sorcellerie—Chimère dangereuse . . .?* (Abidjan, Ivory Coast: INADES, 1979), pp. 87–115, 258–65.

30. *Ceremony*, p. 2.

31. Maurice Dorès, *La Femme village* (Paris: L'Harmattan, 1981), pp. 20–25.

32. *Ceremony*, pp. 132–38.

33. Horne, p. 26.

34. E. P. St. John, *Stories and Story-telling*, quoted in Horne, p. 26.

35. *Storyteller*, pp. 38–42.

36. Claude Lévi-Strauss, *The Scope of Anthropology*, tr. S. Ortner Paul & R. A. Paul (1967, rpt. London: Jonathan Cape, 1971), p. 14.

37. *Storyteller*, pp. 31–32.

38. Ibid.

39. "The Living Tradition," p. 172.

Selected Bibliography

Abel, Elizabeth, ed. *Writing and Sexual Difference*. Chicago: Univ. of Chicago Press, 1982.

Accad, Evelyne. *L'Excisée*. Paris: L'Harmattan, 1982.

———. *Veil of Shame*. Quebec: Naaman, 1978.

Adotevi, Stanislas S. *Négritude et négrologues*. Paris: Union Générale d'Editions, 1972.

Allen, Jeffney. *Lesbian Philosophy: Explorations*. Palo Alto, Calif.: Institute of Lesbian Studies, 1986.

Alta. *Momma. A Start on All the Untold Stories*. New York: Times Change Press, 1974.

Atwood, Margaret. "Paradoxes and Dilemmas, The Woman as Writer." In J. Webber & J. Grumman, 1978.

Ba, Mariama. *Une si longue lettre*. Dakar: Les Nouvelles éditions africaines, 1980.

Barthes, Roland. *Writing Degree Zero*. Trans. A. Lavers & C. Smith. New York: Hill & Wang, 1967.

———. *Critical Essays*. Trans. R. Howard. Evanston, Ill.: Northwestern Univ. Press, 1972.

———. *The Pleasure of the Text*. Trans. R. Miller. New York: Hill & Wang, 1975.

———. *Roland Barthes*. Trans. R. Howard. New York: Hill & Wang, 1977.

———. *A Lover's Discourse*. Trans. R. Howard. New York: Hill & Wang, 1978.

———. *Camera Lucida*. Trans. R. Howard. New York: Hill & Wang, 1981.

———. *Empire of Signs*. Trans. R. Howard. New York: Hill & Wang, 1982.

———. *The Responsibility of Forms*. Trans. R. Howard. New York: Hill & Wang. 1985.

Bastide, Roger, ed. *La Femme de couleur en amérique latine*. Paris: Anthropos, 1974.

Beaujour, Michel. "Flight Out of Time." In J. Ehrmann, 1967.

Bell, Roseann P., Bettye J. Parker, & Beverly Guy-Sheftall. *Sturdy Black Bridges: Visions of Black Women in Literature*. New York: Anchor/Doubleday, 1979.

Benjamin, Walter. *Illuminations*. Ed. H. Arendt. Trans. H. Zohn. New York: Schocken Books, 1969.

———. *Understanding Brecht*. Trans. A. Bostock. 1977; rpt. London: Verso. 1983.

Bernstein, Hilda. *For Their Triumphs & for Their Tears*. 1975; rpt. Cambridge, Mass.: International Defense & Aid Fund, 1978.

Blanchot, Maurice. *The Writing of the Disaster*. Trans. A. Smock. Lincoln: Univ. Of Nebraska Press, 1986.

Blicksilver, Edith. ed. *The Ethnic American Woman*. Dubuque, Iowa: Kendall/Hunt, 1978.

Briffault, Robert. *The Mothers*, 1927; rpt. New York: Atheneum, 1977.

Bruner, Charlotte H., ed. *Unwinding Threads: Writing by Women of Africa*. London: Heineman, 1983.

Burgos-Debray, Elizabeth, ed. *I, Rigoberta Menchu: An Indian Woman in Guatemala*. Trans. A. Wright. London: Verso, 1984.

Cade Bambara, Toni. "What It Is I Think I'm Doing Anyhow." In J. Sternburg, 1980.

Cade, Toni, ed. *The Black Woman: An Anthology*. New York: New American Library, 1970.

Cardinal, Marie. *Les Mots pour le dire*. Paris: Grasset, 1977.

————. *Autrement dit*. Paris: Grasset, 1977.

Cather, Katherine Dunlap. *Educating by Story-telling*. New York: World Book, 1926.

Césaire, Aimé. *Return to my Native Land*. 1956; rpt. Paris: Présence Africaine, 1971.

————. *Discours sur le colonialisme*. Paris: Présence Africaine, 1955.

Cha, Theresa Hak Kyung. *Dictée*. New York: Tanam Press, 1982.

————. ed. *Apparatus*. New York: Tanam Press, 1980.

Chang, Diana. "Woolgathering: Ventriloquism and the Double Life." In D. Fisher, 1980.

Charbonnier, Georges. *Entretiens avec Lévi-Strauss*. Paris: Union Générale d'Editions, 1961.

Chawaf, Chantal. *Rêtable la rêverie*. Paris: Des Femmes, 1974.

————. *Le Soleil et la terre*. Paris: Pauvert, 1977.

Chedid, Andrée. *Visage premier* (poems). Paris: Flammarion, 1972.

Chesler, Phyllis. *Woman and Madness*. New York: Avon, 1973.

Christian, Barbara. *Black Women Novelists: The Development of a Tradition 1892–1976*. Westport, Conn.: Greenwood Press, 1980.

————. *Black Feminist Criticism: Perspectives on Black Women Writers*. New York: Pergamon Press, 1985.

La Civilisation de la femme dans la tradition africaine. Société Africaine de Culture. Colloque d'Abidjan. July 3–8, 1972. Paris: Présence Africaine, 1975.

Cixous, Hélène. "The Laugh of the Medusa." Trans. K. Cohen & P. Cohen. *Signs* 1, no. 4, Summer 1976.

————. *La*. Paris: Des Femmes, 1976.

————. *Vivre l'orange*. Paris: Des Femmes, 1979 (French and English).

————. "Castration or Decapitation?" *Signs* 7, 1, Autumn 1981.

————. *Ou l'art de l'innocence*. Paris: Des Femmes, 1981.

———— & Catherine Clément. *The Newly Born Woman*. Trans. B. Wing. Minneapolis: Univ. of Minnesota Press, 1986.

Clément, Catherine. *Les Fils de Freud sont fatigués*. Paris: Grasset, 1978.

————. *Vies et légendes de Jacques Lacan*. Paris: Grasset, 1981.

Clifford, James. "On Ethnographic Authority." *Representations* 1, no. 2, 1983.

————. "Oneigraphy: A Small Collection." *Sulfur*, no. 11, 1984.

————. "Interrupting the Whole," *Conjunctions* 6, 1984.

————. "Histories of the Tribal and the Modern," *Art in America*, April 1985.

———— & Georges Marcus, eds. *Writing Culture*. Berkeley: Univ. of California Press, 1986.

Corrèze, Françoise. *Vietnamiennes au quotidien*. Paris: L'Harmattan, 1982.

Croll, Elizabeth. *Feminism and Socialism in China*. New York: Schocken Books, 1980.

Dalby, Liza. *Geisha*. Berkeley: Univ. of California Press, 1983.

Daly, Mary. *Gyn/Ecology: The Metaethics of Radical Feminism*. Boston: Beacon Press, 1978.

Davies, Miranda, ed. *Third World—Second Sex*. London: Zed, 1983.

Davis, Angela. *An Autobiography*. 1974; rpt. New York: Bantam, 1978.

————. *Women, Race, & Class*. 1981; rpt. New York: Vintage, 1983.

De Beauvoir, Simone. *The Second Sex*. 1952; rpt. New York: Bantam, 1970.

Deleuze, Gilles. "Intellectuals and Power." In M. Foucault, 1977.

———— & Felix Guattari. *L'Anti-Oedipe*. Paris: Editions de Minuit, 1975.

————. *On the Line*. Trans. J. Johnston. New York: Semiotext(e), 1983.

————. *Nomadology: The War Machine*. Trans. B. Masumi. New York: Semiotext(e), 1986.

Deloria, Vine, Jr. *Custer Died for Your Sins*. New York: Avon Books, 1969.

Derrida, Jacques. *Of Grammatology*. Trans. G. Chakravorty Spivak. Baltimore: Johns Hopkins Univ. Press, 1976.

————. *Writing and Difference*. Trans. A. Bass. Chicago: Univ. of Chicago Press, 1978.

————. *La Vérité en peinture*. Paris: Flammarion, 1978.

——. *Positions*. Trans. A. Bass. Chicago: Univ. of Chicago Press, 1981.

——. *The Ear of the Other*. Ed. C. V. McDonald. Trans. A. Ronell & P. Kamuf. New York: Schocken Books, 1985.

——. "Racism's Last Word," *Critical Inquiry* 12, no. 1, Autumn 1985.

Didion, Joan. "Why I Write." In J. Sternburg, 1980.

Dorès, Maurice. *La Femme village*. Paris: L'Harmattan, 1981.

Dunham, Katherine. *A Touch of Innocence*. New York: Harcourt, Brace & World, 1959.

Duras, Marguerite & Xavière Gauthier. *Les Parleuses*. Paris: Editions de Minuit, 1974.

——. *L'Amante*. Paris: Editions de Minuit, 1984.

Ehrmann, Jacques, ed. *Literature and Revolution*. Boston: Beacon Press, 1967.

Ellman, Mary. *Thinking About Women*. 1968; rpt. London: Virago, 1979.

Etienne, Mona & Eleanor Leacock, eds. *Woman and Colonization: Anthropological Perspectives*. New York: Praeger, 1980.

Fall, Aminata Sow. *Le Revenant*. Dakar: Les Nouvelles éditions africaines, 1976.

——. *La Grève des battu*. Dakar: Les Nouvelles éditions africaines, 1979.

Fanon, Franz. *Black Skin White Masks*. Trans. Charles Lam Markmann. New York: Grove Press, 1967.

——. *The Wretched of the Earth*. Trans. C. Farrington. New York: Grove Press, 1968.

Farb, Peter. *Man's Rise to Civilization*. New York: Bantam, 1978.

Fernea, Elizabeth Warnock. *Guests of the Sheik*. 1965; rpt. New York: Anchor/Doubleday, 1969.

——. *A Street in Marrakech*. New York: Anchor/Doubleday, 1976.

Firth, Raymond. "The Sceptical Anthropologist? Social Anthropology and Marxist View of Society." *Proceedings of the British Academy* 58, 1972.

Fischer, Louis. *Gandhi: His Life and Message for the World*. New York: New American Library, 1954.

Fisher, Dexter. *The Third Woman: Minority Women Writers of the United States*. Boston: Houghton Mifflin, 1980.

Foucault, Michel. *L'Ordre du discours*. Paris: Gallimard, 1971.

——. *Madness & Civilization*. 1965; rpt. New York: Vintage, 1973.

——. *The Order of Things: An Archeology of the Human Sciences*. 1970; rpt. New York: Vintage, 1973.

——. *Language, Counter-memory, Practice*. Ed. D. F. Bouchard. Ithaca, N.Y.: Cornell Univ. Press, 1977.

——. *Discipline and Punish*. Trans. A. Sheridan. New York: Vintage, 1979.

——. *Power/Knowledge*. Ed. C. Gordon. Trans. C. Gordon, L. Marshall, J. Mepham, & K. Soper. New York: Pantheon, 1980.

——. *The History of Sexuality*. Trans. R. Hurley. New York: Vintage, 1980.

——. *Death and the Labyrinth: The World of Raymond Roussel*. Trans. C. Ruas. New York: Doubleday, 1986.

Friedan, Betty. *The Feminine Mystique*. New York: Dell, 1977.

——. *It Changed My Life*. New York: Dell, 1977.

Fukumoto, Hideko & Catherine Pigeaire. *Femmes et samourai*. Paris: Des Femmes, 1986.

Garcia, Irma. *Promenade femmilière*. 2 vols. Paris: Des Femmes, 1981.

Gaudio, Attilio & Renée Pelletier. *Femmes d'Islam ou le sexe interdit*. Paris: Denoel/Gonthier, 1980.

Gauthier, Xavière. *Surréalisme et sexualité*. Paris: Gallimard, 1971.

——. *Rose Saignée*. Paris: Des Femmes, 1974.

Geertz, Clifford. *The Interpretation of Culture*. New York: Basic Books, 1973.

——. *Local Knowledge*. New York: Basic Books, 1983.

Giovanni, Nikki. *Gemini: An Extended Autobiographical Statement on My First Twenty-Five Years of Being a Black Poet*. New York: Viking Press, 1971.

———. *The Women and the Men.* New York: Morrow Quill, 1975.

———. *Cotton Dandy on a Rainy Day.* New York: Morrow Quill, 1980.

Golde, Peggy, ed. *Women in the Field.* 1970; rpt. Berkeley: Univ. of California Press, 1986.

Gould, Karen. "Setting Words Free: Feminist Writing in Quebec." *Signs* 6, no. 4, Summer 1981.

Goulianos, Joan, ed. *By a Woman Writt.* 1973; rpt. Baltimore: Penguin Books, 1974.

Grahn, Judy. *The Highest Apple: Sappho and the Lesbian Poetic Tradition.* San Francisco: Spinsters, Ink, 1985.

Griaule, Marcel. *Conversation with Ogotemmêli.* 1965; rpt. New York: Oxford Univ. Press, 1975.

Griffin, Susan. "Thoughts on Writing: A Diary." in J. Sternburg, 1980.

Groult, Benoite. *Ainsi soit-elle.* Paris: Grasset, 1975.

Halimi, Gisèle. *La Cause des femmes.* Paris: Grasset, 1973.

Hama, Boubou. *Le Double d'hier rencontre demain.* Paris: Union Générale d' Editions, 1973.

Hampate Ba, A. "The Living Tradition." *General History of Africa, I. Methodology and African Prehistory.* Ed. J. Ki Zerbo. UNESCO, Heineman, Univ. of California Press, 1981.

Hebga, Meinrad P. *Sorcellerie—Chimère dangeureuse . . . ?* Abidjan, Ivory Coast: INADES, 1979.

Herrman, Claudine. *Les Voleuses de langue.* Paris: Des Femmes, 1976.

Hooks, Bell. *And There We Wept* (Collection of poems). Privately published, 1978.

———. *Ain't I A Woman? Black Women and Feminism.* Boston: South End Press, 1981.

———. *Feminist Theory. From Margin to Center.* Boston: South End Press, 1984.

———. "From Black Is A Woman's Color." *Hambone,* no. 5, Fall 1985.

Horne, Herman Harrell. *Storytelling, Questioning and Studying.* New York: Macmillan, 1917.

Hull, Gloria T., Patricia Bell Scott, & Barbara Smith, eds. *But Some of Us Are Brave.* Old Westbury, N.Y.: Feminist Press, 1982.

Hurston, Zora Neale. *I Love Myself.* Ed. Alice Walker. Old Westbury, N.Y.: Feminist Press, 1979.

———. *Mules and Men.* J. B. Lippincott, 1963.

Hymes, Dell. ed. *Reinventing Anthropology.* New York: Random House, 1972.

Illich, Ivan. *Gender.* New York: Pantheon, 1982.

———. *Shadow Work.* London: Marion Boyars, 1981.

———. "Vernacular Values." *CoEvolution Quarterly* 22, 1980.

Irigaray, Luce. *Speculum.* Paris: Editions de Minuit, 1974.

Jameson, Fredric. *The Prison-House of Language.* Princeton, N.J.: Princeton Univ. Press, 1972.

———. *The Political Unconscious.* Ithaca, N.Y.: Cornell Univ. Press, 1981.

———. "Third-World Literature in the Era of Multinational Capitalism." *Social Text,* no. 15, Fall 1986.

Jayawardena, Kumari. *Feminism and Nationalism in the Third World.* London: Zed, 1986.

Jones, Gayl. *Corregidora.* New York: Random House, 1975.

Juhasz, Suzanne. *Naked and Fiery Forms.* New York: Harper & Row, 1976.

Kane, Cheikh Hamidou. *L'Aventure ambiguë.* Paris: Union Générale d'Editions, 1961.

Kingston, Maxine Hong. *The Woman Warrior,* 1975; rpt. New York: Vintage, 1977.

———. *China Men.* New York: Ballantine, 1981.

———. "The Coming Book." In J. Sternburg, 1980.

Kishwar, Madhu & Ruth Vanita, eds. *In Search of Answers: Indian Women's Voices from Manushi.* London: Zed, 1984.

Kristeva, Julia. *Des Chinoises.* Paris: Des Femmes, 1974.

————. *Desire in Language.* Ed. L. S. Roudiez. New York: Columbia Univ. Press, 1980.

————. "On the Women of China." Trans. E.C. Kennedy. *Signs* 1, no. 1, 1975.

Laing, Dilys. "The Double Goer." In J. Goulianos, 1974.

Lakoff, Robin. *Language and Woman's Place.* New York: Harper & Row, 1975.

Larsen, Wendy Wilder & Tran Thi Nga. *Shallow Graves. Two Women and Vietnam.* New York: Random House, 1986.

Laure. *Ecrits, fragments, lettres.* Paris: Union Générale D'Editions, 1978.

Leclerc, Annie. *Paroles de femme.* Paris: Grasset, 1974.

————. *Hommes et femmes.* Paris: Grasset, 1985.

Lemsine, Aicha. *La Chrysalide.* Paris: Des Femmes, 1971.

Levertov, Denise. "The Poet in the World." In J. Webber & J. Grumman, 1978.

Lévi-Strauss, Claude. *Race et histoire.* Paris: Gonthier, 1961.

————. *The Savage Mind.* Chicago: Univ. of Chicago Press, 1966.

————. *The Scope of Anthropology.* Trans. S. Ortner Paul & R. A. Paul, 1967; rpt. London: Jonathan Cape, 1971.

————. *The Raw and the Cooked.* Trans. J. & D. Weightman. New York: Harper & Row, 1969.

Lévy-Bruhl, Lucien. *The Notebooks on Primitive Mentality.* Trans. P. Rivière, 1975; rpt. New York: Harper & Row, 1978.

Lewis, Diane. "Anthropology and Colonialism." *Current Anthropology* 14, no. 5, 1973.

Lispector, Clarice. *La Passion selon G.H.* Trans. C. Farny. Paris: Des Femmes, 1978.

Lyotard, Jean-François. *Driftworks.* Ed. R. McKeon. New York: Semiotext(e), 1984.

————. *The Postmodern Condition: A Report on Knowledge.* Minneapolis: Univ. of Minnesota Press, 1984.

MacCormack, Carol & Marilyn Strathern, eds. *Nature, Culture and Gender.* New York: Cambridge Univ. Press, 1980.

Malinowski, Bronislaw. *The Sexual Life of Savages.* New York: Harcourt Brace Jovanovich, 1929.

————. *The Dynamics of Culture Change,* ed. P. M. Kaberry. New Haven: Yale Univ. Press, 1945.

————. *Argonauts of the Western Pacific.* 1922; rpt. New York: E. P. Dutton, 1961.

————. *A Diary in the Strict Sense of the Term.* New York: Harcourt, Brace & World, 1967.

Mansfield, Katherine. "Journal." In J. Webber & J. Grumman, 1978.

Marks, Elaine & Isabelle de Courtivon, eds. *New French Feminism.* Amherst: Univ. of Massachusetts Press, 1980.

Memmi, Albert. *The Colonizer and the Colonized.* Boston: Beacon Press, 1965.

Mernissi, Fatima. *Beyond the Veil: Male-Female Dynamics in a Modern Muslim Society.* Cambridge, Mass.: Schenkman, 1975.

Mikhail, Mona N. *Images of Arab Women: Fact and Fiction.* 1969; rpt. Washington, D.C.: Three Continents Press, 1981.

Miller, Casey & Kate Swift. *Words and Women.* New York: Anchor/Doubleday, 1977.

Mirande, Alfredo & Evangelina Enriquez. *La Chicana.* Chicago: Univ. of Chicago Press, 1979.

Mitchell, Juliet. *Women's Estate.* New York: Vintage, 1973.

Mphahlele, Ezekiel. *The African Image.* New York: Praeger, 1962.

————. *Voices in the Whirlwind.* New York: Hill & Wang, 1972.

Moers, Ellen. *Literary Women.* New York: Anchor/Doubleday, 1977.

Moore, Clark D. & Ann Dunbar, eds. *Africa Yesterday and Today.* New York: Bantam, 1968.

Morraga, Cherrie & Anzaldúa, Gloria, eds. *This Bridge Called My Back: Writings by Radical Women of Color.* Watertown, Mass.: Persephone Press, 1981.

Murasaki, Lady Shikibu. *The Tale of Genji.* Trans. A. Waley. New York: Doubleday, 1955.

Nawal, Yasmine. *Les femmes dans l'Islam*. Paris: La Brèche, 1980.

Nin, Anaïs, *The Diary of Anaïs Nin*. 6 volumes. New York: Harcourt, Brace & World, 1966 (vol. 1: 1931–1934); 1967 (vol. 2: 1934–1939); 1971 (vol. 3: 1939–1944); 1971 (vol. 4: 1944–1947); 1974 (vol. 5: 1947–1955); 1976 (vol. 6: 1955–1966).

————. *Under a Glass Bell*. Chicago: Swallow Press, 1948.

————. *The Novel of the Future*. New York: Macmillan, 1968.

————. *Delta of Venus*. 1969; rpt. New York: Bantam, 1977.

O'Connor, Flannery. "The Nature and Aim of Fiction." In J. Webber & J. Grumman, 1978.

Panoff, Michael. *Ethnologie: le deuxième souffle*. Paris: Payot, 1977.

Paulme, Denise, ed. *Women of Tropical Africa*. Trans. H. M. Wright, 1963; rpt. Berkeley: Univ. of California Press, 1974.

Peckham, Linda. "Peripheral Vision: Looking at the West Through 'Reassemblage'." *Cinematograph* 2, 1986.

Penley, Constance & Andrew Ross. "Interview with Trinh T. Minh-ha." *Camera Obscura*, nos. 13/14, 1985.

Plath, Sylvia. *The Colossus*. 1957; rpt. New York: Vintage, 1968.

————. *Ariel*. 1961; rpt. New York: Harper & Row, 1965.

————. *The Bell Jar*. 1971; rpt. New York: Bantam, 1981.

Propp, Vladimir. *Theory and History of Folklore*. Ed. A. Liberman. Trans. A. Martin & R. Martin. Minneapolis: Univ. of Minnesota Press, 1984.

Qoyawayma, Polingaysi (*aka* Elizabeth Q. White). *No Turning Back*. Albuquerque: Univ. of New Mexico Press, 1964.

Rabemananjara, Jacques. "Le Poète noir et son peuple." *Présence Africaine* 16, Oct.–Nov. 1957.

Raymond, Janice. "The Illusion of Androgyny." *Quest* 2, no. 1, Summer 1975.

Reed, Evelyn. *Problems of Women's Liberation*. 1969; rpt. New York: Pathfinder Press, 1970.

————. *Women's Evolution: From Matriarchal Clan to Patriarchal Family*. New York: Pathfinder Press, 1975.

Reiter, Rayna R., ed. *Toward an Anthropology of Women*. New York: Monthly Review Press, 1975.

Rexroth, Kenneth & Ling Chung. *Women Poets of China*. New York: New Directions, 1972.

———— & Ikuko Atsumi, eds. *Women Poets of Japan*. New York: New Directions, 1977.

Rich, Adrienne. *On Lies, Secrets, and Silence*. New York: W. W. Norton, 1979.

Righini, Mariella. *Ecoute ma différence*. Paris: Grasset, 1978.

Rooth, Anna Birgitta. *The Importance of Storytelling: A Study Based on Field Work in Northern Alaska*. Uppsala, Sweden: Almqvist & Wiksell, 1976.

Rowbotham, Sheila. *Women, Resistance and Revolution*. 1972; rpt. New York: Vintage, 1974.

Russ, Joanna. *How to Suppress Women's Writing*. Austin: Univ. of Texas Press, 1983.

Olsen, Tillie. *Tell Me a Riddle*. 1976; rpt. New York: Dell, 1980.

————. *Silences*. 1978; rpt. New York: Delta/Seymour Lawrence ed., 1980.

Sa'adawi, Nawal el (or Saadaoui, Naoual el). *The Hidden Face of Eve*. London: Zed, 1980.

————. *Ferdaous*. Trans. A. Trabelsi & A. Djebar, Paris: Des Femmes, 1981.

————. *Memoirs from the Women's Prison*. Trans. M. Booth. London: Women's Press, 1986.

Said, Edward. *Orientalism*. New York: Vintage, 1979.

————. "Opponents, Audiences, Constituencies and Community." In *The Anti-Aesthetic*. Ed. Hal Foster. Seattle: Bay Press, 1983.

————. "In the Shadow of the West." *Wedge* no. 7/8, Winter/Spring 1985.

San Severina, Barbara. *Stalking the Evil That's Been Giving Darkness a Bad Name*. Privately published, 1982.

Santos, Emma. *La Malcastrée*. Paris: Maspéro, 1971; Des Femmes, 1976.

———. *L'Itinéraire psychiatrique*. Paris: Des Femmes, 1977.

Sartre, Jean-Paul. *Situations II. Qu'est-ce que la littérature?* Paris: Gallimard, 1948.

Sayer, Dorothy L. *Are Women Human?* Grand Rapids, Mich.: Eerdmans Inc., 1971.

Scheibler, Sue. "When I Am Silent, It Projects." *USC Spectator* 7, no. 2, Spring 1987.

Shan, Sharan-Jeet. *In My Own Name. An Autobiography*. London: Women's Press, 1985.

Shange, Ntozake. *Sassafras*. Berkeley: Shameless Hussy Press, 1976, 1977.

———. *For Colored Girls Who Have Considered Suicide/When the Rainbow is Enuf*. 1977. New York: Bantam, 1981.

Shimer, Dorothy Blair, ed. *Rice Bowl Women: Writings by and about the Women of China and Japan*. New York: New American Library, 1982.

Shostak, Marjorie. *Nisa. The Life & Words of a !Kung Woman*. 1981; rpt. New York: Vintage, 1983.

Sievers, Sharon L. *Flowers in Salt: The Beginnings of Feminist Consciousness in Modern Japan*. Stanford, Calif.: Stanford Univ. Press, 1983.

Signs. Journal of Women in Culture and Society. "French Feminist Theory," vol. 7, no. 1, Autumn 1981; "Feminist Theory," vol. 7, no. 3, Spring 1982.

Silko, Leslie Marmon. *Storyteller*. New York: Seaver, 1981.

———. *Ceremony*. New York: Viking Press, 1977.

Smedley, Agnes. *Portraits of Chinese Women in Revolution*. Old Westbury, N.Y.: Feminist Press, 1976.

Sorcières (Les femmes vivent), no. 7 ("Ecritures") and no. 16 ("Désir").

Soyinka, Wole. *Myth, Literature and the African World*. New York: Cambridge Univ. Press, 1976.

Spacks, Patricia Meyer. *The Female Imagination*. New York: Avon, 1976.

Spivak, Gayatri Chakravorty. "French Feminism in an International Frame." *Yale French Studies* 62, 1981.

———. "Draupadi by Mahasteva Devi." *Critical Inquiry* 7, no. 2, Winter 1981.

———. "The Politics of Interpretations." *Critical Inquiry* 9, no. 1, 1982.

———. "Can the Subaltern Speak? Speculations on Widow–Sacrifice." *Wedge*, nos. 7/8, Winter/Spring 1985.

———. "Three Women's Texts and a Critique of Imperialism." *Critical Inquiry* 12, no. 1, Autumn 1985.

———. "Interview." *Art Network* 16, Winter 1985.

Sterling, Dorothy. *Black Foremothers: Three Lives*. New York: Feminist Press/McGraw Hill, 1979.

Sternburg, Janet. *The Writer on Her Work*. New York: W. W. Norton, 1980.

Thaman, Konai Helu. *You, the Choice of my Parents*. Suva, Fiji: Mana, 1974.

Thiam, Awa. *La Parole aux négresses*. Paris: Denoel/Gonthier, 1978.

Trinh, Minh-ha T., ed. *She, the Inappropriate/d Other, Discourse*, no. 8, Winter 1986–1987.

Trinh, Minh-ha T. *En minuscules* (poems). Paris: Le Méridien éditeur, 1987.

———. *Un Art sans oeuvre*. Troy, Mich.: International Book Pubs., 1981.

———. "Aminata Sow Fall et l'espace du don." *Présence Africaine*, no. 120, 1981. Also *French Review* 55, no. 6, May 1982.

———. "The Plural Void: Barthes and Asia." *Sub-Stance* 36, vol. XI, no. 3, 1982.

———. "L'Innécriture: féminisme et littérature." *French Forum* 8, no. 1, Jan. 1983.

———. "Mechanical Eye, Electronic Ear and the Lure of Authenticity." *Wide Angle* 6, no. 2, Summer 1984.

———. "Ear Below Eye." *Ear* 9(5)/10(1), Fall 1985.

———. "Questions of Images and Politics." *The Independent*, May 1987.

———. "On the Politics of Contemporary Representations." In *Discussions in Contemporary Culture*, Ed. Hal Foster. Seattle: Bay Press, 1987.

———. "Outside In Inside Out." In *Questions of Third Cinema*, Ed. J. Pines & P. Willemen. London: British Film Institute, 1988.

————. "On *Naked Spaces—Living Is Round.*" *Motion Picture*, no. 1, Spring 1986.

————. Script of the film *Reassemblage. Camera Obscura*, no. 13/14, 1985.

————. Script of *Naked Spaces—Living Is Round. Cinematograph* 3, 1988.

———— & Jean-Paul Bourdier. *African Spaces: Designs for Living in Upper Volta.* New York: Holmes & Meir, 1985.

————. dir. *Reassemblage* (16 mm, 40 min.). Women Make Movies (New York); Third World Newsreel (New York); Circles: Women's Film & Video Dist. (London); Idera (Vancouver), 1982.

————. dir. *Naked Spaces—Living Is Round.* (16 mm, 135 min.) Women Make Movies (New York); Museum of Modern Art (New York); Circles: Women's Film & Video Dist. (London); Idera (Vancouver), 1985.

Walker, Alice. "Saving the Life That Is Your Own: The Importance of Models in the Artist's Life." In D. Fisher, 1980.

————. "One Child of One's Own: A Meaningful Digression Within the Work(s)." In J. Sternburg, 1980.

————. *In Search of Our Mother's Gardens.* New York: Harvest/HRT, 1984.

Walker, Margaret. "On Being Female, Black and Free." In J. Sternburg, 1980.

Watts, Alan W. *Nature, Man and Woman*, 1958; rpt. New York: Vintage, 1970.

Webber, Jeannette L. & Joan Grumman, eds. *Woman as Writer.* Boston: Houghton Mifflin, 1978.

Wilson, Amrit. *Finding a Voice: Asian Women in Britain*, 1979; rpt. London: Virago, 1980.

Wittig, Monique. *Le Corps lesbien.* Paris: Editions de Minuits, 1973.

————. *Les Guérillères.* Trans. D. Le Vay. Boston: Beacon Press, 1969.

———— & Sande Zeig. *Lesbian Peoples: Material for a Dictionary.* New York: Avon, 1979.

————. "The Mark of Gender." *Feminist Issues* 5, no. 2, Fall 1985.

Wong, Jade Snow. *Fifth Chinese Daughter.* 1945; rpt. New York: Harper & Row, 1965.

Woolf, Virginia. *Women and Writing.* New York: Harcourt Brace Jovanovich, 1979.

————. *A Room of One's Own.* New York: Harcourt Brace Jovanovich, 1929.

Yamada, Mitsuye. *Camp Notes and Other Poems.* San Lorenzo, Calif.: Shameless Hussy Press, 1976.

Young, Michael W., ed. *The Ethnography of Malinowski.* Boston: Routledge & Kegan Paul, 1979.

Index

Afonja, Simi: on African women and tradition, 114

Africa: propaganda and commitment, 11; power and language, 49, 52; women and westernization, 107–108; women and tradition, 114; griot and griotte, 120, 126, 148; oral tradition and storytelling, 125–26, 148; women and regeneration, 127, 136; women and magic, 128, 136; structure of story, 143

Alaska: storytelling, 125

Alienation: writing and objectivity, 27; anthropology, 58

American Indian. *See* Indian, American

Androgyny: writing, 39

Anthropology: worn codes, 47–49; language and nativism, 49, 52–54; objectivity, 55; as western science, 55–59; as mythology, 59–64; as semiology, 64–67; as gossip, 67–68; as voyeurism, 68–70; as fiction, 70–72; interpretation, 71–73; language, 73–74, 76; compared to history, 84; authenticity, 88, 94; sex and gender, 105; gender and economics, 107; structure of story, 141; cultural anthropology, 157n

Anzaldúa, Gloria: on women and writing, 8; Third World women and difference, 83

Apartheid: ideology and difference, 84; pass laws, 90. *See also* South Africa

Aristotle: defined anthropology as gossip, 68; poetry, history, and truth, 120

Art engagé: Third World literary discourse, 11–12

Assimilation: anthropology, 60–61

Atwood, Margaret: on women writers and sexism, 27

Authenticity: and specialness, 88; and roots, 89–90, 94

Authority: women and storytelling, 122

Awori, Thelma: women and African culture, 108

Ba, A. Hampate: on oral tradition, 126; on speech and power, 127–28, 132

Bambara, Toni Cade: on writing as community service, 9–10, 15; on writing as work, 10; on writing and language, 17

Barthes, Roland: clarity and language, 17; on function of writing, 18; writing and the body, 41; structure of story, 143

Basaa: women and regeneration, 136

de Beauvoir, Simone: women as writers, 18; female identity, 97; difference and the body, 100–101

Bible: women and I Corinthians 14:35, 30

Bir: women and magic

Bisexuality: writing, 39; ear as symbol, 127

Blanchot, Maurice: knowledge and power, 40, 43

Body: women and writing, 36–39; theory and writing, 39–44; as basis for difference, 100

Bricolage: engineer contradiction and anthropology, 62–63, 156n

Briffault, Robert: magic and gender, 128

Brossard, Nicole: on the body and writing, 36–37

Buddhism: reality and language, 61. *See also* Zen

Butwa: women and magic, 128

Cameroon: women and regeneration, 136

Capitalism: women in Gabon, 108. *See also* Economics; Separate development

Cather, Katherine Dunlap: on storytelling and religion, 124

Celebes: women and magic, 128

Césaire, Aimé: on function of art, 13, 15

Cha, Theresa Hak Kyung: on story and storytelling, 119, 122, 123, 126; on truth, 121

Chang, Diana: on writing and authorship, 36

Cheng-tao-ke: verses of and difference, 95–96

Childbearing: images and writing, 37

Children: storytelling, 124–25

China: *yin* and *yang* concept, 67; Julia Kristeva on male/female difference, 103, 116; warrior woman and story, 133–34

Christian, Barbara: gender, 159n

Chuang Tzu: mirror as image, 23

Civilization: storytelling and the primitive, 123–25

Civilized: connotation and storytelling, 124–25, 126, 129

Cixous, Hélène: on sexism and women writers, 27, 37; on writing and author,